DEAR SIS

(CHILDHOOD & ADOLESCENCE)

ABIGAIL OHEMAA AFRIYIE   VICKY OSEI

LUCY AHATTY   ANASTASIA OWUSU-DWUBENG

TINA POKUAAH   EDITH FOSUAH WIREDU

BRIANNA FLETCHER   NATHALIE WANOGHO

MONICA FRIMPONG   ABRAFI AHMED

To
Nina,
May this book
be a
blessing
Love
Ohemaa

ISBN 978-0-9956641-8-0
First Printing 2021

Publisher:
JLG Publishing
www.jlgpublishing.co.uk

Cover Design:
Interlace Media

Website:- www.ohemaaspeaks.com/ladiesinwaiting
Instagram:- _ladiesinwaiting

CONTENTS

FOREWORD

By Byron Kwaning

I'm truly grateful and thankful for the privilege to be one of the first people to read these precious lives of great and strong women. I commend my dear sister Abigail for this masterpiece.

Being predominantly raised by women myself , I already had a special kind of respect for women. But, after reading these stories, my respect for women went to another level words can't fully describe.

This is a book for the records. Whoever reads these stories will be able to testify the realness & authenticity of them, especially how each story unfolds into the great and strong women they have become.

As a Ghanaian, born and raised in the Netherlands (80s kid by the way), I can relate to this book. I think this book is imperative as it talks about life from the perspective of the child, and I think it's important for every parent to read it , to try and understand how their life affects their children's. For children and women, I think this book is an anchor as it unfolds deep secrets and touches vulnerable areas in one's life, which many others might never discover. What this book actually does, is represent the voice of a generation of children and women that go through life and want to be heard and understood.

Just knowing that you are not the only one brings relief to the mind and soul. And at the same time it is uplifting to see how each turns their mess into a message – this requires much strength, maturity, audacity, vulnerability and humility. Thank you, sister Abigail, and to all the writers. I love and respect you for your stories shared. It offers the reader many perspectives to the reader.

From a male perspective, I do want to commend all women who helped work on this masterpiece and I commend all women who will read it. I am a product of a strong, hardworking and loving mother, so I can't stress enough on the level of respect I have for women. What I have noticed in some of the stories, if not all, is the impact of a father/man in a household, whether absent or present.

Its saddening but at the same time motivating. The sad part is how many men/fathers, those supposing to be the head, take certain decisions which scars the household for life. And what makes it even worse, is that the household never gets invited into their world of thinking and feeling because they simply don't share. The motivating part is that reading this book as a man - besides the fact that I grew up without my biological dad and not having the relationship that I so much desire to have - I became exposed to the importance of fatherhood. The ramifications of reluctant fathers stand out for me and it pushes me more to be the best husband and father I can possibly be for my wife and children. I get to learn from the mistakes our parents made and I have the opportunity to do it better.

My prayer is that every man that reads this captivating book will understand and never undermine their role as the head. That they will know that it's not just about the things you say or do that can be painful but sometimes it's the things you did not mention or do that can bring even more harm. I want to be part of the generation that will be present as a father in every aspect (socially, mentally, academically, financially and most importantly spiritually).

I want to thank God for the fathers as well, as many have tried their very best, but probably didn't know how to cope with the changes they had to endure.

The variety of stories make it a dynamic & unique book and it is worth reading every page. Personally, this book hits home for me and I pray that as you read this book, may it influence you and your home positively.

Love & Blessings
Byron Kwaning

OPENING PRAYER & STATEMENT

Heavenly Father. Thank you for the gift of writing. Thank you for never forsaking me during the hard seasons in my life. As all these stories are present in the book, I pray that women worldwide would be able to identify themselves with each story and gain insight into their own childhood to help either themselves or people around them.

DEDICATION

Dedicated to every young girl who was not listened to in their childhood.

Dedicated to every person who had a different childhood who have not expressed themselves.

Dedicated to every person who hid and felt that their childhood was embarrassing, weird and shameful.

Hard times don't last, though people do.
May this book give you the peace you need.

Rest in Eternal Peace Uncle Kwaku Nyamekye, thank you for encouraging me that I have a voice.

To my Daughter Anayah: from my womb you gave me the strength and courage to write my story. Mummy loves you.

OHEMAA'S ACKNOWLEDGMENTS

Firstly, I want to thank Almighty God for bringing me this far and for me giving this vision to have to the courage to speak about my life journey.

I'm eternally grateful for the strength God has given me in this season because without His unfailing love I wouldn't be here.

My mum Agatha Manu aka Sister Yaa,

Understanding you as a child was difficult but now, I get it and you're the strongest woman I know.

Thank you, mum, your pain will never be in vain.

Love you always.

My Dad Ralph Boakye – Mensah,

We are still growing and even though we might not get things right all the time, it's okay. It's part of the journey.

My Siblings,
    You pushed me to be on a different level.

My nannie Linda,
    Thank you for showing us that there was a bigger world outside of the estate. I will always appreciate you.

My teachers at Notre Dame:
    Mrs Williams
    Ms Shaw
    Ms Pennant
    Ms Christine
    Mrs Arrowsmith
    Ms VO

Goodness these teachers made a massive impact in my life during my school days, especially when I came back from Ghana.
    So much was going on at home when I was 15 and these teachers made school a safe haven for me.
    They believed in me like no other and drove my passion for the subject English in an indescribable way.
    I am Grateful for Great teachers.

The late Father Tom Heneghan,
    Without Father Tom and his prayers and his kind words that helped my faith, I wouldn't be where I am today. You will never be forgotten; we all still miss you dearly.

My fellow Sisters on this book project,
    Book 1 is finally here. I'm grateful for our sisterhood, we are stronger together.

To Family and Friends who have supported me on this journey I'm extremely grateful, God bless you.

Last but not least, my Husband Kofi Tawiah Mensah,

You were not there at the beginning but since you came, you have motivated and encouraged me to be the best that I can be.

Thank you for your love and patience I appreciate you so much x

1

ABIGAIL OHEMAA AFRIYIE – MY PREPARATION

My Preparation.

It had always been mum, me and dad. Looking back at the pics I looked like some posh child. I matched with everything. When it came to Church and family hall parties, my parents didn't play; I was always looking on fleek. My earliest memory is my aunty putting a baby within my arms. I remember a few minutes after, I complained that the baby was heavy and I then proceeded to ask my aunty when the baby was going home. My aunty replied that she was here to stay and that she was my new sister. I was absolutely devastated and replied that I did not want a sibling.

From that day I had this baby around me, following me, everywhere I went; from that day onwards, I knew my life would be different.

What a time it was, breakfast time. A full English breakfast, beef sausages (when they were in fashion, now not currently because of mad cow disease.)

Now those days, the mirror newspapers would do giveaways in the Saturday newspapers, where you could win from as little as £5 to £50.

Now £5 was a lot in the 90's: it could buy a lot, unlike now.

Now let me explain my routine. My dad worked nights and my mum worked during the day, a nine to five. My dad always joked that I was the one that "made him" work nights. His story was that when I went to my childminder's place who was Asian, Indian to be specific, I came home speaking the Indian language, which he particularly was not happy about as I had not even started speaking his national language Twi. That's when he took it upon himself to get a night job. I mean I'd/I would believe his story, as whenever he speaks about it, he speaks with such emotion.

So, dad took me to school and picked me up for a while. He was at all my school meetings and even became a school governor and he was honoured to open our new primary school that was rebuilt.

This continued until I was about seven and a half years old.

Suddenly things changed within the household. Things became loud. The breakfast mornings faded out, my parents would speak their native tongue heavily and never taught myself or my sister so we could not understand. As fast as I was, I learnt Twi and taught myself, funny enough. I used to put a glass cup to the wall almost every night to listen to my parent's conversations and eventually I picked up everything. I would let my sister know some things, I was careful not to tell her everything, as it was my duty to protect her. It was just that at that moment I didn't even know what I was protecting her from.

Time went on and things got worse. The shouting became loud, violence occurred and most times I was in the middle shouting for it to stop and at the same time making sure my sister was not able to see anything. gosh it was tough.

1997 was the year when the problems grew. You see, mum got made redundant and received a huge pay packet; all I remember was peeping and seeing numbers.

The family and particularly one of her siblings had her eye on this and that changed everything. Honestly from that day it was like a spirit of destruction walked into my house and took control. It went from family members taking my mum, myself and my sisters to these

Pentecostal churches to get redemption -as apparently my mum has turned "mad overnight"- to my parents, myself and my sister going to Ghana mid 1998 for a massive family meeting, where my parents got divorced.

Ghana was not a strange place to me at all. My parents made sure of that from the age of three. I mean at eight years old I knew the language; I knew I was from the Ashanti tribe and I knew pretty much most of my family members in Ghana.

This trip was not like the others. My uncle (my dad's brother), whom I was close with, joined us on the trip before he moved to USA and we stayed at my dad's other brother's house where we normally would stay.

All was calm at first, and then my mother's family came one Saturday morning to have a family meeting, which seemed to go alright.

But the very next day, the Spirit of destruction came and brought a few friends.

An argument sparked up and to the life of me, I don't know what it was about. The next thing my dad and a few of his family members from his paternal side, were hurling insults at my mum and dragging her and pushing myself and my sister out of the house. They threw us out like dogs, like we were worthless, and one of the family members drove us somewhere really far. A place where no child in fact no human being should be. This place was dark, people were lying around, some people were bleeding, people were talking to themselves, people were drugged…it was hell on earth. Mum kept us close and told us not to worry. My sister became hysterical, and I could see the fear in my mum's eyes whilst she was reassuring us. I took it upon myself to shield my sister and hug her tight and often closed her eyes to everything.

I felt that we were there for ages. My mum would pray fervently and made sure we prayed with her. She also said that our faith would get us out and it truly came to pass. We were there for a few days until this pastor could see that we were not like the rest. I got to realise that it was like a church camp for people who were outcasts.

Just like that we were sitting outside, and I could hear one of mum's brothers, my uncle Kwasi, and he was demanding to see us. I nudged my mum and told her I had heard my uncle's voice. She rose up and my uncle saw her, and he demanded that she get our stuff and go. He was picking us up.

What a miracle! We found out later that my mum's side of the family were looking for us and didn't know where we were, until my dad's family member confessed.

Once we left that God forsaken place, the next thing I remember is me, my mum and sister being on the flight back to the UK. My dad and my uncle were also present on the same flight.

I knew the divorce was final when we returned. Mum went back to work the next day. Dad stayed away and came to the house whilst mum went to work.

He literally emptied the flat and took everything with him, EVERYTHING, including the sofas; the house was bare apart from my room I shared with my sister.

I just remember sitting in the middle of the corridor with my sister who did not have any clue about what was going on and kept asking me why is everything that was going on, like, why didn't Dad say bye? I was eight years old, what could I say? I just told her to sit with me and I cuddled her and got her dolls to play with.

Later that evening, Mum returned to a practically bare house but never showed us that it affected her in any way. She was concerned that we were ok.

Mum did her best and literally bought everything new from scratch and within a month everything was replaced.

After that ordeal, things became quieter and loads of questions were asked, especially at school: "Where is your Dad?"

-Life with mum as a single parent

I mainly attached to my dad in my early childhood and I honestly thought I was getting to know my mum again. Boy! I got to know quickly that she was tough and sharp, she didn't play around. She let us know that just because she was a single parent she wasn't going to be deemed as "soft."

Mum did very well. She was a hard grafter and worked hard to provide everything for myself and my sister, and if she couldn't afford the latest Nike trainers for us, she would do something extraordinary to make us smile and we would quickly forget about the Nike trainers we wanted.

We continued to go on holidays and 1999 was the first time we went to the land of the brave, the USA. It was the best, we had so much fun.

Just as we were settling down as a single parent household, when holidays would occur, mum trusted me enough to stay in the house and look after my sister; I mean it was pretty normal for kids to be left alone in the house. Mum would prepare our food and put it in containers and as she had showed me how to use the microwave, all I needed to do was warm the food. It was safe to be honest. We were told not to open the door to anyone, and that we must not answer the house phone unless it was the designated times that she would call.

Me and my sister had a blast : we watched movies on VHS and watched all the Disney movies, *"Look who's talking"* and *"Coming to America"*, just to mention a few. We were banned from watching a certain movie and I mean my mum would put the fear of God in us, telling us she would know if we would had watched it.

The movie in question was "The Colour Purple". Mum thought we were too young to watch and understand it and I can honestly say I obeyed and never watched until I became seventeen years old..

Everything was going well. I was enjoying this single parent household.

Dad came over a few times and we went to his house a few times, but the bond was broken and mum particularly didn't have anything positive to say about him whenever he was mentioned. So within time, we didn't mention him much.

Fast-forward to our summer holidays back in 2000, we stayed at home until mum came back at 3PM.

.   .   .

Before I talk about my household dynamics, I want to talk about my environment.

I grew up in a very diverse area and everyone was like a family and everyone jelled.

My estate was in the middle of 4 estates and we would come together, vibe and joke around. The elders in the areas were highly respected and they looked out for us, individually. The genre of music those days were RnB and Garage, so when Solid Crew came on the scene, they put South London on the map and that was a moment in history.

This day was a bit different. Around 1PM there was a knock on the door and this knock wasn't any normal knock. It was more of a banging noise which couldn't be ignored. As per usual, myself and my sister sat still, thinking the person would go away. Far from it! The banging noise turned into loud voices and drilling sounds, and before we knew it, police and social services were in our corridor and found us in the living room.

I was flabbergasted and shocked as in why they were here.

The one thing I remember asking the social worker, was how she knew/ had known we were here alone. She then said to me that my mum's sister had reported her. As young as I was I didn't understand how my Aunty was able to do that, when I specifically remember my mum asking her several times if she could look after us during the term time because she had to go to work in the evenings, and my aunty always refused. Yet, she was the same one calling social services on her sister. Wow.

Social services took us away, and we stayed with a foster carer for a bit until we got to stay with a family member nearby.

Social services were in our lives and that was the tip of the iceberg that sent my mum over the edge - from that day, coming home and not seeing her children being home triggered my mum and she ended up being sectioned for depression.

The Spirit of Destruction came again.

Things died down, mum got released a few weeks later and we were reunited with her. This happened again the next summer, which was strange.

In July 2001 we were able to move to a new apartment which was in the same estate and I felt that it was new fresh start for all of us. No more bad memories in our previous house and it was figured by the professionals that mum would not be trigged.

2001 July we moved, and things got better, mum had got a new job and the holidays continued, laughter had filled our home, I finally had my own room loool

Mum was a staunch Catholic and went to prayer meetings every Tuesday

Whilst all this happened, my sister and I became the subject of gossip and we were shunned by our own Ghanaian community. There is nothing I have not heard before to be honest, very hurtful things, but I vowed I would show these people something one day.

2001 July we moved, and things got better, mum had got a new job and the holidays continued, laughter had filled our home, I finally had my own room loool

Mum was a staunch Catholic and went to prayer meetings every Tuesday

Fast-forward towards the end of 2002. A week after my birthday in November, mum went to her prayer meeting. I was a teenager so it was fine and as the prayer meeting wasn't far from the house, mum would go from 7:30PM to 9PM.

This Thursday was different: 9:30PM passed and mum wasn't home. 9:45PM passed and she still wasn't home. My heart started beating fast and I didn't understand where she was. Those days my mum didn't have a mobile and it wasn't compulsory to have one like it is today.

I heard a knock at the door at 10:15PM. I opened the door and it was my neighbour who lived on the first floor and a police officer, but I honestly did not panic at all. The worry on my neighbour's face did not faze me either. I remember the police officer asked me what my mum was wearing and I recall laughing and describing my mums coat and saying that my mum used to say that the coat was older than me.

The policeman then said they found mum and that she was in the ambulance downstairs ready to take her to the hospital. At that point, I felt my knees turn to jelly and as my sister was still sleeping, all I could think to myself was how I was I going to tell her.

I quickly took the house phone and called my older cousin Yvette and explained everything, and the police reassured her and my Aunty that they would bring me and my sister right away to their house.

I remember waking my sister up and packing a few clothes. We were driven in the back of a police car; my sister was so exhausted I do not think she registered what was going on.

We got to my Aunt's house and they hugged us tight.

My sister and I went to visit mum on the Sunday with our church members. When I saw my mum I didn't even recognise her at all. I tried to stare at her, but I couldn't as the wounds on her face were horrific. She had blood shot eyes and she was totally unrecognisable. I had to control my emotions and comfort my sister, as she was hysterical and didn't even want my mum to touch her. Now that part was sad, and I could see the sadness within my mum eyes which was unbearable to watch.

Mum got released from hospital a few days later and when she got home it wasn't any easier at all. My sister was adamant that she did not want my mum to check up on us during the night and that made mum cry. Tt was an emotional time. I constantly heard my mum tell an Aunty that she was in disbelief that her children were scared of her because of her facial injuries.

Time passed on and mum's wounds started to heal, but I was not prepared for the announcement she was about to make a few weeks later.

Mum started moving things around. It didn't make sense at first until she sat me and my sister down and explained that by Christmas 2003, we were moving to Ghana for good.

Oh, hell no I was not having a bar of it! I really thought of it as a merely small idea my mum had, which I could influence. Hmmm boy was I mistaken. I did everything in my power to stay: I got social services involved and I begged family members to help my mum see reason but it did not work. I remember breaking the news to my friends at school first and they were as confused as I was. Everyone knew that you only got sent back to the motherland for bad behaviour, but here I was, a top student who was going back for good.

The very day, I bid farewell to my peers on my estate, and it was emotional. Most of the men showed up with some of the girls and we were all trying to hold in the emotions. I was leaving my life behind to go and live in Ghana for good, I didn't know what to expect.

On the 19th of December 2003 we arrived at Kotoka Airport in Accra. Now my mum is not a woman to joke with at all, when she says she is going do something, she sticks to her word.

As I mentioned earlier, I'm not from Accra, I'm a pure Ashanti girl and those days the transportation to Kumasi was not how it is now. Mum wanted to get to Kumasi ASAP and we landed quite late in the night. Mum asked a taxi driver how much he would charge to drive us and our luggage to Kumasi. I personally think that the taxi driver thought it was a joke and smiled at first, until he saw my mums face. He quoted her a price and before you knew it, we were on our way to Kumasi.

Okay, check this out. Let me do a little back story on this o you can fully understand this part. The previous year we had come to Ghana on a holiday and mum had communicated with my dad's side of the family to vacate the family home, as she was taking full ownership of the house. My dad's side of the family agreed and said that they would vacate the family house within that year. As we stayed at our house, various conversations were held about which school we would go to and where.

After the Christmas period we went to various schools and mum was very adamant that she did not want us to cut our hair, so eventually we ended up going to Roman Girls.

I mean school in Ghana is a whole different experience, let me walk you through it. Well before I do that, let me introduce a friend called Linda who lived nearby. She went to St Louis JSS (Junior

Secondary School) and always came by in the morning. I, she, and my sister would leave the house around 6:30AM and our normal routine would be to climb a steep mountain near the mosque that was close to our house. We would sing Ghanaian Gospel songs on our way to the Tro-tro station. Our favourite artist at the time was Esther Smith. When we got to the Tro-tro Station it was literally survival of the fittest, meaning you had to rush and quickly get the right Tro-tro. It was crowded that morning and I mean my sister found it tough; she got her dress caught so many times on the Tro-tro door.

Let me be honest: my mum did ask me if we wanted a driver to take us to school and I refused on the grounds that I didn't want everyone thinking we were some rich privileged kids from the UK. It was important that I was srrn as a normal child like everyone else.

Anyway, once we got back to school, we had to go put our bags down in our seats. Once the bell rang, which was at 7:45AM, we had to line up in our form class groups and sing the national anthem when the principal came downstairs - (I mean I didn't know the words, I was miming. Trust and believe I learnt the words fast by the end of the week, I didn't want no problems!)

Then a teacher went around checking everyone's nails and if your nails even had a speck of dirt in them, you would have to go to the front of the school and receive your punishment.

After we went to class, and I must say my classmates were different but amusing, they were fascinated by me and I surely was fascinated by them.

Lunchtime was interesting, rice and stew in a polythene bag. I mean... I was used to a canteen hall with plates and cutlery, but I didn't care to be honest. I enjoyed it with my new friends. They were mostly amazed that I knew how to play "Ampe", which is a popular children's game in Ghana. My mum taught me in London. In Ampe, a leader is chosen and he or she stands opposite the first opponent. They both jump up, clapping and kicking one of their feet forward. If the leader has put the same foot forward as the opponent, the leader wins a point and moves on to the next player. If the feet are different, the opponent becomes the new leader. Someone keeps score and the first person to reach a pre-determined number of points is the winner.

After school, myself, Linda, my sister and a few friends would walk through Bantama to Kejetia to get a Tro-tro home and we would sing popular hip-life songs, especially VIP- Ahomka Womu, which was the popular song at the time. As we got settled in, my sister and I became popular around the area. I mean, we were the only British kids.

I was extremely close with my Fante neighbours: we would go and watch TV with them, as we were still waiting for some of our stuff from London to be shipped. The culture in Ghana was so much different to London. For example, at that time, abortion was common amongst schoolgirls, people were drinking concoctions with broken glass and male teachers asked students to bring homework or anything as small as a Supermalt to their house so they could have their wicked way with the students.

I received letters from a few of my friends from the ends and I do remember before leaving, asking my friend Keisha to do her best to find my dad to get him to get me back. To be honest, I didn't think she would make it happen, until she sent me a letter explaining she found my dad and that he was coming. I wrote her back explaining that I wanted to stay and that I became comfortable. She was not happy with my decision and pleaded with me to hear him out as he was coming to Ghana soon.

I didn't dare utter a word to Mother, instead I told my sister and asked her what she wanted to do.

She practically was like: "Whatever you want to do". She would follow me.

It was a tough decision, a real tough one. When I look back now, I feel bad for planning my exit but at the time I slept on it and realised that if I didn't take this chance I would miss out on my GCSE's. I had already started the process when I left at my peak in Year 10.

Ok, so what I did was pack mine and my sister's bag and got my two friends to help me. They were my sidekicks and even though they didn't want me to go, I gave them some of my treasured belongings to remember me by.

Before that I had met up with my Dad in town and I told him of my master plan, which he agreed to. All he had to do was park the car. He secretly knew I was able to pull it off.

That very day, it was a Saturday and my mum would go to the market. Once she left, we decided to move out but it was not as easy as you think. Picture this scenario:

Mum leaves the house around 7AM. I wake up my sister to start getting ready. Those days no one relied on phones, so when you tell your friend to come at a certain time, they will arrive. I had already packed our bags the night before and put them underneath our bed. I couldn't take everything so I had to make sacrifices. My friends Rukayaa and Jalia came on time to the house and arrived around 7:45AM. They secured the premises to make sure no one was coming around. I had to negotiate with them, and as I didn't have any money, I gave them some of my treasured belongings for them to remember me by. They appreciated it. 8:30AM, my sister and I were ready. I promised myself not to look back, otherwise I would have second thoughts. At 8:45AM we left the house and at the top of the hill my dad was waiting in the car. When my dad saw us, he helped us immediately and took our belongings. Me and my sister hugged Rukayaa and Jalia and wept quietly as we left.

The evening we left we knew our mum was looking for us, as my late uncle Kwaku had made contact with my dad. Thankfully mum knew where we were because my uncle told her later that evening. My master plan came to pass, but with one major hiccup that I had forgotten about. Our passports. I know I was not the only child that did not have hold of my passport; I personally feel it's an African household mantle, where the parents hold your passport until you leave the house. After so much prayer and pleading, mum invited me, my sister and dad back to the house. When we arrived, she gave us a hug and gave my dad a stern look. I began to plead my case with my mum but she kept saying that we were going back to London soon. I gave my sister the look to plead with mum, as I knew that that would be mum's weakness. Eventually mum gave in and gave our passports to my dad but she did not do so without giving my dad the wickedest warning, and trust me, I saw the fear in my dad's eyes.

Fast forward to us arriving in London with our Dad. It was a breath of fresh air until quickly realising that I and my sister were not the only children. Yes: we found out that we didn't just have one sibling but two (twin siblings) and a step mum, and we all had to sleep in one room.

If I'm honest about the situation, my twin siblings didn't have a clue. I mean they were only 2 years old at the time and they were excited and embraced us, especially the twin girl.

We also met our new stepmom and it was so weird. She was welcoming at first until she saw me and my sister as a threat.

The first time I realised that my step mum saw us as a threat, was when we went back to Stockwell to see our friends and family. She mentioned to me and my sister that we could take as long as we liked. We only had to make sure we came back at a decent time.

My sister and I were not disobedient at all and we came back to our Aunt Janet's house on time. Our step mum was jovial with us and applauded us for coming back on time.

When we reached back at the house, it was a different story. Our step mum lied to our dad and said we came back late. She exaggerated the story and made us look like we were disobedient. That evening our dad scolded us and I remember very well my sister crying on my shoulder, saying to me: "Should we have stayed in Ghana?". I replied to her saying, "No we made the right decision." and reassured her to go back to sleep.

That very night I cried myself to sleep, I would never show my sister that I was fearful but to be honest, that day was just the beginning of our nightmare.

A few months after, we moved out to a temporary accommodation in Norbury and we started going to our school again. I was blessed to start Year 11 straightaway without having to repeat Year 10, as I had only finished one term.

Going to school was like a holiday getaway because things were getting worse at home. Our step mum became evil by the minute. She would insult us when our dad wasn't around, speak to our mum and reassure her that she was taking care of us. When she finished the phone call, she was emotionally abusive to us and insulted our mum. We did not retaliate; we would ignore her and cry in our rooms.

It honestly felt like our dad was under a spell and whatever she said to him was golden. She stopped cooking for us and when I would cook, she would sometimes ban me from the kitchen and me and my sister had to wait till our dad came home before we could eat.

The worst part was that she turned our three and four year old siblings against us whilst my dad was at work.

School became my paradise; I loved English Literature and Music.

I sang in school competitions and assemblies and my passion for singing was my way out my reality. I would stay at after-school clubs and utilise the library like no other, just not to have headache at home. I had to do all the housework, I would sing my Ghana Gospel songs that were on cassette tape. It helped me so much, till this very day Ghana Gospel touches my soul like no other.

Family and friends had no clue what was going on, I was too scared to speak up. I just had to keep going.

I had no idea that God was hearing my cry for help until one afternoon, my step mum was on the phone to her younger sister in Ghana and per usual insulting myself and my sister. But this phone call was different. She started talking about my dad and started ridiculing him, and that took me by surprise.

I don't know what came over me and what courage I possessed that evening but when my dad came home, I asked to speak to him and he sat down and I explained everything that my step mum had said on the phone to her sister. Honestly, looking back on it now, it felt like a Nollywood movie, with all its gimmicks and sound effects. Suddenly, my dad looked at me in horror and hugged me and immediately went for my step mum and started packing her bags. There was a huge argument and my stepmom did something out of madness: she called the police and made it look like my dad had assaulted her, when he didn't. Police came and didn't take her seriously as myself and my sister backed up our dad.

Shortly after that, we moved to our permanent residence, but it was only I, my sister and my dad.

My dad had split up with my step mum and as much as my dad wanted the twins to join us, our step mum refused and she moved to the other side of London to her sister's.

Life was just getting better and I felt more at ease in our new place. No wicked step mum around, I mean I was able to breathe again.

The only pressure I had for myself was waiting to receive my GCSE results and to decide which college I wanted to go to.

My mum learnt of everything that had happened and was astonished. Fast forward a few weeks later, she came back to the UK and stayed with a family friend around the corner from our new place. Mum explained that she missed us so much and that she was staying for the summer holidays and that she would go back to Ghana.

When my dad learnt that my mum had moved back to the UK, he was a bit uneasy and started acting different. And, instead of him talking about it with myself and my sister, he resulted to anger.

I was washing up a pot in the sink, the fufu pot to be precise, and I had just put boiling hot water with washing up liquid in the pot when my dad walked in and asked why the pot was not washed. I replied that the pot needed to be soaked. That's when my dad put my right hand in the boiling water and as I screamed, my sister walked in, and before you knew it I was in a corner huddled up as my dad was hitting me with a bag full of kitchen items. I cried and screamed so loud that I didn't even hear the knock on the door. Within a few minutes, six policemen were in our flat arresting my dad and picked me up from the floor. I had cuts and bruises on my legs and my sister clung to me crying.

My mum was called immediately and she became hysterical within the hour. We were dropped to our family friend's house and were asked to stay there for the time being.

I was limping for 10 days and had a cast on my knee for the pain.

My mum, who had not planned to stay in the UK, decided to stay after the incident.

We were placed in a hostel in Brixton Acre Lane and shared a room. It was fun. Even though we were cramped, we were all united again.

Family members from my Dad's side kept calling to plead with me not to press charges. Tt became too much all at once but my mum convinced me not to press charges and look forward to a brighter future, and I listened.

A few weeks later, I passed my GCSE's and got great results. I got into the college I wanted, to study American History, Law, and Sociology.

Later, we moved again to another temporary accommodation, a flat where I got my own room. Finally.

I was finally free and when I turned 17. Life, I thought, was beginning ooo! I was heavily raving (clubbing) from Friday to Sunday, bear in mind I was working and going to college and still made it on time. Those days I was receiving EMA payments, I even paid for my first holiday with friends at 17. We went to Greece to live it up. I was enjoying myself loool.

At 17 I was already in a relationship with my first boyfriend who I lost my virginity to. To be honest, in my day, 17 was late. Lots of my peers lost their virginity at 14-16. Nevertheless, I thought I was lit. T-Mobile had Mate Rates and 5-Day Passes those days, which allowed you to call T-Mobile numbers for free for £5 for 5 days. The good old days. I was enjoying myself so much I didn't even notice that my mum was spiralling until 14th February 2007 to be precise, when the door was knocked down ferociously and my world turned.

OHEMAA'S GOLDEN JEWELS

The ends taught me a lot about myself, I felt safe and protected. The ends were the first place I learnt to smoke a joint and roll up. The ends is where I learnt to fight, to ride a bike and the ends is where I learnt about loyalty and dance loool.

When I look at my journey and especially this part of my life, it felt like a movie. I never valued my self-esteem and it was low. I didn't value myself one bit, I just kept going through trial after trial and never did I once think about myself.

I had to be firm; I had to be strong,

I once drew for paracetamol pills and looked at them in a different way, luckily, I came back to my senses and put them back.

I was drowning, I didn't know how to keep myself above water and only caught myself whenever temporary joy was around.

Some advice to stepmothers or stepmothers to be: be yourself, don't do too much. Remember your role and take it with grace. No matter how frustrating the situation can be, always remain loving.

I remained transparent so that I was heard and seen, so that you may see too.

Speak your truth for it belongs to you

Psalm 91 is my dedication to this part of my story, a Psalm my mother taught me never to forget.

"He shall cover thee with his feathers, and under his wings shalt thou trust: his truth shall be thy shield and buckler."

Psalms 91:4 KJV

VICKY'S ACKNOWLEDGMENTS

Foremost, I would like to thank God for His faithfulness in my life and for guiding me through writing this book. I would like to express my gratitude to Abigail Mensah for giving me the opportunity to tell my story, and for her support and encouragement during this emotional journey.

Besides Abigail, I would like to thank all the other ladies who have participated it has been beautiful working alongside such strong women.

My sincere thanks go to my family and friends who have played an important role in my life and kept me going.

Lastly, to everyone whom I have encountered who has inspired me, prayed for me and kept me smiling. I dedicate this book to the reader, I hope that that whoever reads this can identify and be inspired to identify the load you have been carrying, protect your peace, seek self-healing, give yourself forgiveness, love and grace in wholeness.

Sis, you got this!
Vicky Osei

2

VICKY OSEI – SIS, YOU GOT THIS

S is, you got this.

Knowing that you overcame before and can overcome again, don't let challenges cause you to believe you are abandoned by God, it leads you to look for love in the wrong places. Romans 8:37 states: *'No, in all these things we are more than conquerors through Him who loved us.'*

God gets us through the difficulties in life, these battles brings out the champions in us. At a comma moment in your life do you put a question mark, exclamation mark or a full stop?

Shortly after I was born, my mum and dad split up and my dad *moved* back to Ghana. So, it was just me and my mum and it was not easy for her as a young single mother who had been living in London just over a year. I still bear the scar today of the hard times we went through. Later, my mum met a new man and had my brother. The relationship didn't work out and she kicked him out. My mum, being a first-generation immigrant in London, did her best to ensure I had a happy upbringing. She never had anything good to say about my dad and my dad used to tell me 'Don't be like your mother, study your books!' (he especially shouted this in public) .Being stuck between the two of them was not one of my fondest memories.

My dad came back when I was around four years old. I was pretty much a daddy's girl and he always wanted me to be happy. He would buy me nice things whenever I spent the weekend with him (and whichever girlfriend he was with), and he would show me off to his friends. Even today my dad has stories for days about his time with me in London (for some reason he's still obsessed with Piccadilly Circus). When I was eight years old, he moved out of the country to start a new family and we grew distant. I used to think my dad never loved me enough to come back for me, and at times I thought maybe if I was a boy, he would be closer to me. We never spoke about why this happened, so I blamed myself.

As a child, I was the 'golden child' other parents would ask their children *'Why can't you be like Vicky?'* (yep, I was that girl!). All I knew was to just do my best and anything I wanted my mum would get for me. Me, my mum and my brother had a lot of fun (thank you mum!) Despite being a young single mother of two, she never showed us her struggle. I didn't grow up in a strict home, so I was a free thinker - in fact when I made the ridiculous decision to Jeri curl my hair at nine, my mum allowed me (really mum? Really??) Two weeks later my hair fell out and I was taunted by my brother for months for looking like a boy!

Before I started secondary school, my mum met my *second* stepdad. I always felt uneasy about him and after she had a child by him (and later two more), I confronted him about his real intentions with my mum. However, I was shut down by my mum and was made to apologise, no conversation. Having a new stepdad changed the dynamics at home, things weren't as fun and I found myself doing all the chores and helping with the children, so I never spent time playing outside with the other children. My stepdad didn't play a father role to me and my brother, so I played more of an older brother to my junior brother, given he didn't know who his father was and had no role model. I had no room to be me. I had no one to express my true feelings to and at the same time I didn't understand what I was going through. Me and my brother did a lot together and I developed a love for the things he loved: football, wrestling, games and rap music. Looking back, this is where I suppressed my feminine energy and became more of an authoritative and masculine person at home. This stuck with me even into my adulthood. I saw my value in providing support for my family and being strong. When I got my first part-time job, I made contributions to the home without question.

Identity is what we find hard to grasp, and it comes from understanding who our parents are and how they saw us. Our parents are giving us a 'good life' because that is that they wanted for themselves. We see a lot of things they go through and the things that happen, but we don't understand why these things happen and it's because we lack understanding. It's when we grasp that understanding at our mature age that we can identify the issues and the impact it has on us. As the first born I took on a huge responsibility to help my mum but I also took it upon myself not to be a daughter or a sister. I developed a layered armour, pushing my issues aside and focusing on others.

In secondary school I was described as one of the smartest students and as the class clown! I was always known for making people laugh (and I was the face you avoided if you had to do a reading in assembly). I remember being suspended from lessons on April fool's day because of a prank gone wrong! I also had my serious side to me; I was diplomatic and serious about studies but I was very welcoming and friendly which made me a likable person. I didn't have a best friend, but I had a group of close friends. However, I was not good at telling people how I felt. I had a temper but would mask it with silence or laughter. I had a good relationship with my friends, but I never addressed my emotions. Looking back, a few have said it was hard to read me unless I was always laughing. This is because I was struggling with who I was. I couldn't identify Vicky because I suppressed who I should have been and showed people who they wanted to see.

I dreamed of becoming a paediatrician and although I was given an offer at Southampton University to study medicine, I didn't make the grades to secure my place and I felt my whole world come crashing down as I didn't want my plan B. Studying medicine was the only way of showing I had made it, making everyone proud of me and having one of my goals ticked off! I went home and cried, the reality hit me that you don't always get what you want, and I felt like a disappointment. My friend encouraged me not to give up and guided me in applying to Kent University to study Biomedical Science through clearing. It subsequently led to the career I am in today and I have no regrets!

I'm sure you have noticed I don't mention much about God, but I still had faith in God. When I was a child we never went to church but through my curiosity, I attended church with friends and even played the lead role in the 'Good Samaritan' for the church play. I would pray to God and always talk to Him. I lived my childhood looking to God as my 'dad', as my dad wasn't around to speak to. But I never saw myself through God's eyes and did not know my identity. People perceived me as confident and strong, but I didn't trust anyone to help me, I wanted to be in control. I would be supportive to others and be the problem solver. Carrying strength for others is where I felt valued even though the load was too much for me. I didn't want people to see that I was struggling and I associated this with being a disappointment and being weak, so I would only tell people of my issues once I had solved them.

Expressing real emotion was hard for me and I would often dismiss expressing them. Looking at my attachment personality, no surprise I'm the Dismissive Avoidant! Amongst the myriad of family issues over the years, not being honest with myself and not knowing who I was in Christ, it was in my late twenties through counselling that I found out the effect this had on me internally. I had to learn to accept myself, accept the heavy responsibility I carried as the eldest and a female, accept my imperfections and accept that I am ever evolving into a healthier state of mind. I wish I had more compassion on myself and if I was to take myself back to when I was eight years old and tell my inner child that it's not my fault and not my responsibility, then I would readjust my crown and smile.

. . .

My mum wasn't a church goer until my late teens, she was more interested in the famous pastors who would visit from Africa or America. A pastor told her that her family members including her children were possessed by demons and this completely broke our home. She was convinced that her family was the reason for things going wrong in her life and she would constantly say hurtful things and pressed us to 'confess'. It led to a fight with my stepdad and they split up. One day my mum told me to get ready and that she was taking me and my siblings somewhere. We arrived at a pastor's house......

I've left it there until part two!

VICKY'S GOLDEN JEWELS

What keeps me going? Knowing that I overcame before and can overcome again, don't let challenges cause you to believe you are abandoned by God. Examine and pay attention to your attachment personality and to how you communicate with others. Look at your upbringing and the culture you come from. We are social beings and thrive on connection, so identifying that trauma you have been through is the first step to grace, self-healing and working towards your wholeness.

LUCY'S ACKNOWLEDGMENTS

I would like to take the moment to thank Destiny for giving me the courage to tell this story. Also, my friend turned sister, Abigail, whom I have known since secondary school. Over the year I have learned so much from you and we have grown together. I would like to thank Lara and Helen L. During this stage you both play a crucial part in my life and at young ages were so caring.

Also, my mentor Natalie, in our short time of mentorship, you have encouraged me and helped me step out of the box. Without you I don't think I could have actually finished writing.

And to the girl, boy, woman, man reading this. You're just at the beginning, your time is not over.

3

LUCY AHATTY – LETTER TO MYSELF- FROM ME TO YOU

Letter to myself – from me to you.

My first memory of life starts around the age of four, I lived with Nanny Pat in Somerset, Southwest England. Nanny Pat was a white elderly lady who took many children in. Despite this memory being vague I can recall it as being nice. I had three meals a day and other children to play with. However, moving back home to South London there was something missing. I could not fault my mum at the time, as she was busy working multiple jobs to ensure I never had to work but also to support her family back home. And the truth of the matter is that I never lacked; with the time that she had off, my childhood was full of designer items, eating in fancy restaurants and shopping all over London.

Whilst my mum was busy working, I had to grow up and be independent from a young age. I taught myself to fend for myself, but I found it very lonely. One occasion while in primary school around year 1, I went to school on my own though this was not allowed/legal. The school called home to tell my mum off for allowing me to come to school by myself. When she picked me up, I remember my mum hitting me on the head with something so hard that it bled. From that day I had to go home with different people, or should I say different "aunties", until I could attend after-school club. In primary school, I was always causing mischief and craving attention from the teacher. This got me into a lot of trouble and it significantly impaired my learning. I remember reading my first book at the age of 6. Reading was such a struggle but I wanted to read, because I knew that learning would be my freedom. In year 3, I changed primary school; I found it hard to settle in. I felt like an outcast because everyone had their friendship bubbles from reception and there was me coming in at year 3. Eventually though, I did make friends. My behaviour did not change much when I changed primary schools, I still struggled with my learning which made me destructive in the classroom. My destructive behaviour combined with my constant bed wetting ended up with me seeing a child psychologist. My memory is quite vivid of this but I do remember attending a hospital and being asked multiple of questions and being given toys to play with.

My first memories of my Dad was when he lived in Old Kent Road. He would come and pick me up and I would spend the day with him. He was a cool guy I guess; I could not fault him as he was not really around that much. What was prevalent to me at the time was that my mum and dad had a tonic relationship; which was maybe based on the fact that he had remarried. My dad had remarried a lady who had a daughter who was a few years younger than me, he went on to have a further two children. It was ironic when I ended up in the same primary school as my stepsister, which did not end well. We argued in school and this caused tension, especially because we used the words of our parents, "your mum stole my dad", etc. Looking back, I could only imagine what the poor girl had gone through. She must have had her own past with her father, yet another man had come into her and her mother's life and his ex and daughter were causing trouble. The trouble between my mum and dad and his new family had deep-rooted effects. I remember one day specifically that my dad came to pick up my stepsister and walked past me, ignoring me. This tormented me for years and even now, when I sit back and think about this situation, I wondered why my mum took me to that school. Was it to spite my dad? I was caught in-between the battle lines rather than being protected. Collateral damage in their spiteful breakup!

With so much confusion going on in my young life, I was vulnerable. Primary school is where I first experienced sexual abuse, with "uncles" touching my private parts at a young age. I found it weird, but I didn't tell anyone. Was this normal? At a later age, maybe age 6, I remember one of my nanny's children trying to engage in some sort of sexual encounter. This very memory is very clear, and I remember him showing me his penis and trying to tell me to drink his semen. I refused, I later told my mum and she called him to the house. I remember vividly that she threatened to call the police and I think she exchanged some strong words with him. I never went back to that house again. These sexual encounters did not arouse me but at the time I blamed my mum completely.

In the summer holidays before secondary school started, my mum was granted her indefinite stay after 11 years of being in the UK. We flew to Nigeria and that's when I met my older brother for the first time. My brother was 4 ½ year older than me, he was small in stature and looked the same age as me. We could not relate much to each other but while I was excited to not be the only child, our cultural background caused us to clash.

When we returned from Nigeria, my mum went to university and I started secondary school. This is where my freedom began to increase. I recollect a tenant who lived with us for a while and tried to have sexual encounters with me on many occasions while my mum was out. He would give me money and even at that age I learned to manipulate him to get anything I needed, including writing letters to school. My mum later returned to Nigeria in November 2000 and left me with an aunt in Peckham who was strict but taught me values. During my time in her house, I started going through puberty and I remember telling my mum, but I felt she had no interest at all. We were becoming strangers. Eventually, my brother from Nigeria came to live with us around the beginning of September 2001. I remember this clearly, because it was around the time of 09/11. My brother and my relationship continued to clash; I saw him as this African boy and he probably saw me as this spoilt English girl. Despite this, it was nice not to be home alone anymore with weird tenants and also have someone to talk too. Not long after, he moved out as his and mum's relationship deteriorated.

My relationship with my mum continued to be a strain, turning into physical fights and me spending more and more time outside. By summer of year 9 I started hanging around with the area locals. One day we all met up and went out to play. There were about 7 girls and we all got spilt up by the boys, one of whom took me to the block and took my virginity. I didn't even know what I was doing or what virginity was. I remember going home wondering what had just happened. It was horrible! My belly was in pain, it was so fast and so raw. I was so naïve! The guy I lost my virginity to was lovely, he wanted to be my boyfriend, but I had no idea of what a relationship looked like. I spent that summer in the streets whilst my mum was away in Nigeria again. She left me with my grandmother who spoke no English, which left me having no regard for her. She could not control me. Sex was nothing and I had no feeling towards it. Is this what I saw on the TV? That summer all we did was have sex, partied and repeat. Never once did I have a voice. By the end of the six-week holiday I became ill. I ended up in the hospital. I remember the Doctor in A&E saying I was pregnant. I was in denial and ran away from the hospital and went home. I wanted to die, I was just 14, what was I going to do? Every day I banged my belly hoping it would go away and it did not. Despite my friends from the area wanting to be there for me, I became isolated from the world. I felt this was my problem and I had to deal with it, and I did not want to answer any questions. The sickness and nausea from the pregnancy felt like I was paralysed, and I was so weak that I could not do anything. I eventually ended up in hospital. The irony of this was that I ended up on a children's ward. A memory I try not to conjure, is when my mum came back from Nigeria, and the hospital refused to let me go home. I will never forget the look on her face when she walked through the door, the first day she came to visit me. She had tanned dark skin from the sun and big pearly white eyes, she was wearing African millennium braids and a brown jacket, the shame really came to shower me that day. Plenty of discussions were held with regards to my welfare, even in which my dad and his wife were involved. They all asked me what I wanted to do; I just kept quiet. Discussion about an abortion happened - which I think was steered by my mum - in which I agreed.

After meeting and meetings, it was concluded that I would have an abortion, however, I refused to go back home with my mum or go stay at my dad's, choosing instead to going to foster care. I think this was merely due to shame and I did not want to go home and be insulted. I went to a foster home in Lewisham, I was commissioned to still go to school which I did for one day but continued to have sickness. My social worker and school agreed for me to stay home till my abortion. Foster care was very much a simple life, I had a room and an allowance. Eventually, my mum persuaded me to come home just after a week of being in foster care and a week before my abortion appointment. On the day of my appointment, I remember the drive to the clinic and me sitting in the back holding in my sickness and my mum just insulting me all the way. I had opted to go under general anaesthesia, I wanted it to be over and done as quick as it could be done, and no pain endured. And that's what I got, I went to sleep and woke up and it was over. They told me the procedure was easy with no complications, however, I needed to take antibiotic for a suspected STI. I was able to go home the same day. I returned home and the first thing I did was that I vomited and cried it was over. I became numb to pain and feelings, but my life could go back to normal.

My head teacher welcomed me back with opened arms. We spoke about my abortion and how I felt, and she referred me to counselling, which I felt at the time was the best thing for me. I found that my school was my safe place. I got a pass for acting up in class and would go and sit with the head teacher. I think they understood the damage that had happened. I had weekly talks with the counsellor, but it took me a long time to speak. In many sessions we would just sit and stare at each other, I don't think I ever told her the full story of my abortion, we mainly spoke about school. As for me the abortion was a distant memory that I had locked away.

Life moved on. I was not interested in boys and became distant friends with those in my area. My relationship with my mum continued to worsen. I would run away and go on a bus ride for hours, even over night to avoid being at home. When I decided to return home, the police would come to my house and threaten me that they will put me in a secure unit, but I didn't care. I wasn't scared. After all I had tasted the forbidden seed. I tried to stay at my dad's house, but my mum would always persuade me to come back home.

Every time I would return home for a period, I found security in church. I went to a Catholic church near my secondary school and also a Pentecostal church in Peckham. Every day I was at my mums I would wake up early and go to the 7 AM mass and then go to school. During this time, I joined the church choir. By the time I was entering year 10, my mum and I had fought so much that I ran away and was picked up by social services. I remember going into a children's home. I continued to go to school and engaged in my studies. It was the only thing keeping me sane. I enjoyed my time at the children's home because I had freedom. I had my room, and my weekly allowance and people to talk to. We cooked together on weekends and the workers would help me with my work. I thought I was going to stay there till I was 16. But one day, I came back from school and my social worker was present. I was told I had been found a placement with a family. I was upset and refused to go, I barricaded myself in, screamed, but ultimately was forced to go by the police. I spent 7 months in a foster home with a Caribbean lady. I remember the first day I got there, my social worker went through my history with her and the look on her face said it all. I had a box room and there were two other foster kids that were sisters living there as well. The Caribbean lady was nice most of the times but I found her to be sometimes rude, which caused her and myself to clash. One Friday night I ended up having a big clash with her, and it ended up with me getting removed by social services and getting taken to an elderly lady's house in Croydon. That day, I walked into the house and put my stuff down in one corner and left immediately. I ran away and stayed at my friend's house with her mum over the weekend. I was honestly so grateful to have somewhere peaceful to lay my head. By Monday, social services were at school waiting for me. I got taken to another home in Croydon, where I got on with the lady who gave me my much-needed space.

I remained there just under a year and just before my GCSE; I went back home to my mum's house. I left secondary school with 7 B-C GCSE's! My headteacher and other teachers were so proud of me. I ended up going to a college in West-London to study 4 A-levels. College was okay at the beginning but to be honest, I could not focus and ended up dropping out because I was once again having issues at home. I got myself a part-time job to keep me busy. By September I decided to go back to a college in Croydon but this time, I had moved out of my mum's house to stay with my friend because the environment at mum's was toxic. Eventually, I was placed into a hostel. My own space, I loved it. During my time at the new college, I made new friends, including Lara, who then was and has remained a crucial part of my life. I looked up to her. Lara had a different upbringing, she came from a good home, with lovely parents and was very caring. She invited me into her home. I remember one night while we were out, she met her best friend who later became my boyfriend.

He had stolen my number and called me when I was alone. He chased me and he was persistent in it. I was not interested at first but with his persistence, I fell deeply for him. He became my first official boyfriend and things moved so fast between us. We were inseparable. He stayed at my hostel most of the time. His relationship with his mother was strained which might have been what we had in common. At first, Lara was not happy about our secret relationship, in which I did not blame her, after all, he was spending most of his time with me. I started skipping college, as I didn't not know what I wanted to do next in life, and became preoccupied with my boyfriend and work. During the summer, my boyfriend started to change, he started to spend a lot of his time with a new crowd that eventually were going to change his life. One Friday night, he dropped me off at Helen's house (the one I ran away to during secondary school), gave me a kiss on my forehead and said I should call him when I was ready to go home. I didn't hear from him again. I called him over the course of the day leading into the weekend. This was not of his character; I knew something had happened. That Sunday night he called me and told me that he had been arrested, and had to go court the next day. He told me he was going to be at the court at 07:30, and in my naivety I went to the court house at 07.30 and waited till the doors opened up at 09:30. I waited the whole day to find out that he would be remanded in custody. That night, and all the next day I cried.

I am 17 years old and pregnant again, and the father of my child is in prison, what am I going to do?

LUCY'S GOLDEN JEWELS

Do not rush through your younger life. The bible talks about time: Ecclesiastes 3:1-8

There is a time for everything, and a season for every activity under the heavens: a time to be born and a time to die, a time to plant and a time to uproot, a time to kill and a time to heal, a time to tear down and a time to build, a time to weep and a time to laugh, a time to mourn and a time to dance, a time to scatter stones and a time to gather them, a time to embrace and a time to refrain from embracing, a time to search and a time to give up, a time to keep and a time to throw away, a time to tear and a time to mend, a time to be silent and a time to speak, a time to love and a time to hate, a time for war and a time for peace.

Use your time wisely. Friends will come and go but your future is yours and it's important. The path you are on right now may not be ideal or what you have planned. But in TIME, believe and you will see.

ANASTASIA'S ACKNOWLEDGEMENTS

I want to thank the Almighty Father for giving me the strength and inspiration to write and talk about His word. Thank You for guiding me in the right path of peace and salvation. I am grateful that through the life experiences He has provided me with, I am now able to motivate and inspire someone out there.

My dear husband Mr Dennis Owusu Dwubeng. The love that you have continued to show me, and our children is immense. Your words of encouragement have been my motivation. You are my confidant; my best friend and I pray that the Lord will continue to make our love and bond grows stronger. I appreciate you so much my darling. I love you.

My sons Nathaniel and Nickell, I love you both so much. You have helped to me to become the woman that I am today. I have learnt so much from being your mother. You have brought me so much joy and happiness and I pray that you will both grow up to fulfil the purpose that the Lord has ordained for you. I love you dearly my sons.

My parents Mr Frank and Mrs Joyce Osei-Bonsu. I have seen how hard to you have both worked over the years just to provide me with the best. I appreciate and love you both dearly.

My brother Nana Yeboah. Biggy! As I call you. Bro you have

inspired me so much and I am so proud of everything that you have accomplished. Love you bro.

My Spiritual father Apostle Isaac Gyamfi Yeboah. God bless you for all your words of wisdom and advice. I am grateful for your life. God bless you.

Prophet Francis Biney. Another inspirational man of God in my life. God bless you for all your efforts.

Mrs Abigail Mensah. This woman here is the definition of love. My sister and friend. I thank God for your life, and I thank Him that He is using you to build a ministry which is a great inspiration to many women worldwide. May the Lord bless you in abundance.

The God Mothers of my children, Abigail Mensah, Abena Opoku, Jessica Manu and Michelle Darkwah. Thank you for being a great inspiration to your godchildren. We love and appreciate you so much.

My sisters Fiona Osafo, Josephine Kensah, Kirby De-bords, and Christabel Aladetoun. You have each helped, encouraged and supported me in so many ways. The love I have for each of you is immense and I pray that the Lord will continue to provide many opportunities for blessings to fall upon your lives.

All my friends and family who have a wonderful presence in life. Thank you for all your love and support. God richly bless each and everyone of you.

4

ANASTASIA OWUSU-DWUBENG – MY SUPPORT SYSTEM

My Support System.

Growing up as a teenager in a Christian home in the millennials with two Ghanaian parents, was interesting to say the least.

Would I say it was challenging? In some regards, yes and in some aspects no. I would say my challenge turned into a life lesson.

My father travelled from Ghana to the UK in 1962. Some may say he might be quite westernized considering that he had been living here for 40 years. When I was growing up as teenager, however, he held on strongly to his Ghanaian values. He was very passionate about where he came from, being from the Ashanti tribe, and he made sure that this transpired onto his children. One thing I must say that my parents instilled me, is to never forget my roots and to have in depth knowledge of my heritage. This included knowing about my family background, speaking our mother tongue and my mother teaching me how to cook traditional meals and how to carry myself as a well-trained Christian woman. My mother is a devout Christian and he would take me to church every Sunday. I grew up in the Methodist denomination, however, due to life experiences and self-development, I moved to a Pentecostal church.

Okay, as I mentioned earlier, were there some challenges? In some
ways yes.

So, here's a bit more about my family setup. My household
consisted of myself, my big brother who was born in Ghana but came
over to stay in 1992 and my father and mother. I have a half-sister but
she lived elsewhere with her children. So, you can imagine the
dynamics of having a British born Ghanaian and a Ghanaian born,
who are 9 years apart in age. Was I close with my brother? Yes, I was,
although being born in Ghana, he understood my temperaments and
in return I understood him too. So here was the challenge, although
my parents had been living here for many years. It's fair to say that
some characteristics are not adaptable! Like the saying goes: a leopard
never changes its spots. For example, I had many secondary school
friends, but my parents were very selective of who was allowed inside
our home. Having friends of the opposite sex was deemed a taboo
until I reached college, as it was mixed gender. For me at the time, I
found this quite annoying and I didn't understand why my parents
were being so hard-headed. My brother in turn also adapted to the
"British" way of living very quickly, and my parents struggled to
understand why, since he had only been in the UK for a short period
of time. I remember there was a time when my brother went to play
football with his friends but didn't inform my parents, and when he
got home, I think we all know what happened next. With African
parents, I believe that the teenage years are very important to them as
they believe that is what shapes the children into adults. In Proverbs
22:36 it states, "Train up a child in the way he should go; Even when
he is old, he will not depart from it."

In their eyes, an unstable teenager equals an unstable adult and it
is their priority to ensure that this doesn't happen. Going back to the
challenges I entailed growing up as a teenager, I would say that it was
always linked to my choice of friends. Whoever knew me then, and
now, knows that I am a friendly person, always wanting to help where
I can. However, I do believe this has caused me much pain in my
adulthood, I will get to that later. I remember always having some sort
of fear within me when asking my parents if I could go to my friend's

house or if in turn a friend could come over. It would always result in some form of lecture about "Afekubo" a Twi term for unnecessary friendships.

It usually left me feeling quite down and wondering if my parents wanted me to have friends at all? When I started university at the age of 18, I would say that this was the beginning of my learning curve when it came to friendships. A lot of people let me down in my first year and I spent many months feeling quite isolated, even though I was surrounded by people that seemed to care. But it did give me time to realise it was more than just about friendships. Tt was time for me to love myself more: "Anastasia you need to know your self-worth and value."

I believed in God but I wouldn't say that my Christian life was the greatest. I was still far from God but I did start to look more towards Him, especially in my final year when I was commuting from home to university and I had more time to reflect on who I was as a person, even though I still had a lot of work to do.

So onto the non-challenges, one thing I have to praise my parents for is their encouragement and support during my education from secondary School through to university. I can proudly say that I wasn't one of those children who were hounded by their parents to be a lawyer or a doctor. My parents always wanted me to follow my interests. I have vivid memories from being a little girl, my mother bought me a musical VHS called *"Popskool"* which showed children singing the hits from the 70s and 80s. I had such a burning desire to be part of it that my dad actually travelled to the address of the production company, only to find out they no longer existed. Knowing that my interest was around singing and acting, he enrolled me into drama school at our local theatre, which I attended for many years and stopped at the end of Year 6. From then on, my parents always knew I would study something media related, and I went on to study Media at A-Level at university. I remember the joy in my parents' faces when I graduated and I also in turn showed gratitude to them because they allowed me to be me and study what I loved. I currently do not use my degree to work as I am now a primary school teacher, but I am happy that I was able to embark on a journey in education where I wasn't pressurised or compared to Aunty Aggie's daughter who was studying to be doctor.

I am grateful to my parents for the support they showed me and, myself, being a mother now, I will also ensure that children follow and utilise their talents and also make it known to them that we are born uniquely and will walk different paths in life.

So as I reflect on my journey through adolescence, I am grateful for the ups and downs. I have learnt to love myself but most importantly I have learnt to put God first in everything that I do, and that I am a priority when it comes to life choices.

When I reflect, my parents were very right. We have to be mindful of the people we accept into our lives. Matthew 7:16 states, *"By their fruit you will recognize them. Do people pick grapes from thorn bushes, or figs from thistles?"*. The scriptures tell us to love our neighbour as we love ourselves but we need to be able to define who is for us, who will bring us goodness, blessings and not deceit and this is something that I have had to learn the hard way. Growing up from my teenage years to adulthood, I have let various types of people into my life and I have suffered many scars from this. From going out of my way to do good unto people, only to be repaid with ungratefulness and disloyalty. I have let many people into my home, into my heart and into my world.

I have to come realise that we need to protect ourselves. People come in and out lives carrying different spirits and agendas, we need to seek Christ first in any decision we make. We need to study, take time and analyse people before we go ahead and make them influential in our lives.

People change throughout their life and while spending 24/7 together in school/college may have been essential, it's ok to grow more independent and want to explore separate paths. This does not mean we should disassociate ourselves from people as there are amazing people out there, and I can honestly say I have a closed few who I can gladly calls sisters and brothers.

ANASTASIA'S GOLDEN JEWELS

What would I say to my younger self?

Pray over who you allow into your heart and into your world. Not all that glitters is gold, you need to have the spirit of discernment.

Remember your self-worth and value, we are all human but carry different characteristics. Associate yourself with people who love and value you for you.

"But blessed is the one who trusts in the Lord, whose confidence is in him". JEREMIAH 17:17

TINA'S ACKNOWLEDGMENTS

First and foremost, God I thank You for simply being You, thank You for Your love, Your grace and Your mercy. You have a way of restoring us like nothing ever happened. Finding you was the best thing that ever happened to me. Abigail, thank you for being obedient to God's calling over your life, for bringing us all here together, for making this happen, for being a part of our healing. Last but not least, thank you to my amazing family and friends, I could not have done life without you. To every individual that has spoken life into me, every individual who has been part of my purpose, I love and appreciate you all.

5

TINA POKUAAH – INFLUENCES

I nfluences.

Have you ever wondered how different your life would have turned out to be had certain things not happened? This question has intrigued me for as long as I can remember. I often found myself wondering whether my life events are happenstance or part of a divine plan. However, as I matured spiritually, I learnt to rely less on my own human intuition for answers and instead place all my focus on seeking the true voice of God. This had a positive effect on how I responded to the life-altering events which have shaped my life journey.

So, I begin this exploitation of my 31 years on this earth with one of my favourite scriptures, "Before I formed you in the womb, I knew you, before you were born, I set you apart; I appointed you as a prophet to the nations." Whenever I find myself in the middle of an unexpected storm or when nothing seems to be going according to plan, I mediate on this verse and suddenly all the fear and anxiety is subsided. I become calm and feel at peace, knowing that the God I serve is limitlessly powerful and will direct my every step until I reach my divine destination.

Before I dig deeper into my spiritual journey, it is important to me to give you an insight into how I came into this world.

My mother unexpectedly gave birth to me in January 1989, on a day she had just visited the doctor for her regular prenatal check-up. However, on this occasion, things did not go as originally planned. She recalls walking into the doctors room for her 11.30AM appointment, to then surprisingly waking up later on a hospital bed in the presence of friends and family, giving her the news that her baby girl was born at just 26 weeks. As a result of an eclamptic fit, the doctors had to perform an emergency caesarean to save both mine and my mother's lives.

During our time in the hospital, she suffered extreme blood loss, caught pneumonia, and had to be cautious of the levels of her blood pressure. However, as the scriptures say, God's grace is truly enough for us: 3 months later my mother's health improved tremendously, and her little warrior baby was now stable enough to survive without the assistance of an incubator. There were, however, some concerns that my language development might be delayed, hence why I attended regular appointments up until I was 4 years old. The positive changes in my growth were now becoming more apparent and the doctors were confident that I had reached the same developmental level as other 4 year-olds.

Knowing that I had a 50/50 chance to live, I think more ways than one have changed my outlook on life. It has taught me gratitude and the absolute importance of being determined and persistent, even in the face of adversity. I grew up in circumstances which on paper would have considered me 'vulnerable', as I was from a black working-class single parent family residing in an inner-city area. However, I never really lacked. Being the baby of the family, I guess I was kind of spoiled and although my father never lived with me, he was always a part of my life. My mother has always been a strong and resilient woman and ensured that I followed suit. Growing up we attended a Methodist church which I enjoyed for the most part. I eagerly waited for Sunday to arrive so that I could meet with my church friends and take part in all the fun activities, mainly singing and dancing. But when I now reflect on the time I spent at church as a young girl, I realize that I never had a real relationship with God; I just knew he existed, otherwise who else would have created the world?

As I moved up to secondary school, I attended church less and less and the gathering of friends, singing and dancing took place in a new environment, in the neighbourhood or at the clubs. I grew up in an area where it was normalized to be exposed to street robberies and the mandem selling drugs. There was one occasion when a neighbour of ours had got hold of a gun, he was so excited about it and when I failed to share the same enthusiasm, he held the gun to my head. A few months after, he then advised me to stop hanging outside of my house as a rival gang were after him. His reason was simply that he did not want me to be an accidental target to a drive-by shoot out. That was the reality not only for me but for many young people in my area. I recognise that for many young people getting, involved in gang culture may not be a personal choice but one driven by other circumstances beyond their control, such as lacking a supportive and safe home.

However, I am extremely grateful that my family were my safe and supportive haven and that I took a key interest in my education and enjoyed learning. Even though I was never quite set on exactly what I wanted to be, I always knew the kind of woman I wanted to become. This, however, did not mean that I didn't get into trouble every so often at school, for either having a bad attitude, getting into fights and even being expelled from school in Year 9 for 'inciting violence'. I enjoyed the hype of hanging out with the elders, was attracted to the bad boys and thought I was mature enough to be in a committed relationship at 16 years old. Interestingly, I somehow managed to find a balance between having fun and dedicating time to my studies. As a result, I was able to achieve good GCSEs and proceeded to the next stage of my educational journey without difficulty. I enrolled to do my A-Levels but failed miserably gaining 3 U's, which at the time was a huge disappointment. The importance of being determined and remaining persistent even in the face of adversity had been deeply engraved in me and because of that, I had no choice but to pursue with my studies regardless. Although I had always been the "baby of the family", my parents were not letting me off the hook that easily. I had no choice but to work extra hard making sure that I secured a place at university. My grades did not get much better in the second year and I only got a place at university through clearing.

TINA'S GOLDEN JEWELS

So I walked through life, confident that I could do it on my own terms, not knowing that in the next chapter God was going to truly humble me, leaving me with no choice but to run into His arms for strength and refuge… Many are the plans in the mind of a man, but it is the purpose of the Lord that will stand. – Proverbs 19:21.

EDITH'S ACKNOWLEDGEMENTS

Writing this piece was not easy, as it took me back to my childhood. It reminded me about a lot of things, things I had buried somewhere in my heart.

To God be the glory, I am a changed woman. I am new yet I have a story to tell. My story which is not only mine to tell. I want to acknowledge some precious people around me. Because this story was just a small bit of me, I just want to acknowledge just a few people who played a major role in my life.

First of all, Almighty God! The one who I run to with my problems, and the same God who I run to when I am overflowing with blessings. The same God I have doubted so many times, yet He forgives me over and over again. Thank You for LOVING me and APPRECIATING me.

My parents! I really thought about how to say this, but they are two individuals who need their own acknowledgement just for having me as their child! But they have been the pillar without knowing. My other half Manfred, I could write a whole book about you. My baby! The support from him alone is just indescribable no word can justify! God gave me what my heart desired. And I just want to thank you for choosing me! And trusting me. I Love you.

My MPOM Oh the shining stars of my household! The 4 little angels who can keep me up all night without fail and also be the first to wake me up, I would not change you for anything! Because I believe strongly that you are the ones behind my strength. Without my children I don't know how I would do certain things.

Abigail Mensah without a fail! The one behind this idea! The sister who came in my life so late, I even asked God before, 'Why?' But you know what? God knew why! How to say I appreciate you to someone who has made a great impact on me is an understatement!

'EElimiteD'. Now you are thinking group names? Eunice & Denise, the two most elegant, intelligent women I know. God knew I needed women like them around me. Pure positivity! God bless you both for understanding me. And loving me the way I am.

My J's and mummy's. The J's are my everything! My blood who are there at every little step that I take! I can write a lot about my own family! Jeffrey, Joel, Joycelyn, Jefflyn, Josephine and Mummy the words for her I can't put it on paper! God will bless her so much .

Awuraadjowa. Hmmm my dear, you came in my life at the start of my journey at 17/18 years old, but what we have gone through God has really been faithful and I am so grateful to have you in my life. I have a whole lot more people to thank but for this part of my life, I guess this is it

6

EDITH FOSUAH WIREDU – IT BE YOUR OWN

IT BE YOUR OWN.
     Growing up in a city within the Western world was normal for me. My parents, however, are from Ghana in West Africa, and as I never lived in Ghana, it's quite difficult to compare their lifestyle to mine in West.

As a teenager, I became a bit rebellious and always wanted to do things my way. I looked for love in the wrong place as my emotions were all over the place.

Little Yaa, or should I just say Edith, which is the name in my passport. I was born into a household where my father left my mum and I due to his own personal issues. Life has a funny way of showing you things you would never expect; little did I know my dad would play a major role in my life. Growing up I was known as the quiet girl, I never once started a fight or even fought at primary school. I was that girl and friend who would watch others fight and probably take you home after your fight or I would hold your stuff while you were fighting. It was not necessarily because I could not fight, but I generally never looked for trouble. Until I got into real trouble later on in my life...

I have been raised by my mother pretty much my entire life. We had a close relationship and I was always with her. Growing up in a flat in the south-east part of Amsterdam was great; I had a great childhood that I cannot complain about. At a young age I attended church but I attended several churches and did not stick to one church. There were times that I attended church with other friends and family, until I was about nine years old when we started attending the church which I am still attending till date, "The Church of Christ", Amsterdam branch.

As I became a teenager, I was everywhere, I just became loose. I was just all over the place, emotionally and mentally. When I look back at myself, I do not know why or how, but as far as I know I did what I wanted and looked for love in the wrong places. Looking for love in the wrong place led to me losing my virginity and doing things I should have waited until marriage, or perhaps not even have done at all. I now realise that I was looking for love. A fatherly love. When I was younger, I didn't realise that I needed fatherly love, as it was the norm that my mother represented both parental roles. And it did not occur to me, until I reminisce about the choices that I made, and now that I'm an adult I now know that I was craving the love and the attention of a father. I never fully understood why my father was not around, all I knew was that he was absent in my life. Whenever I asked about him, the story changed over the years. At first it was that he had gone away and would be back, and then it changed to him passing away.

Little did I know... I found out that he was locked up in prison and his release date was a mystery. Until that day I got a call from my aunty.

On the day I got the phone call it was spring, and I remember sitting outside and chilling with my friends. My aunt mentioned to me on the phone that I should pass by her house, this was nothing out of the ordinary as I went to this particular auntie's house very often, so I did not think anything about it. When I got there, I greeted my aunt and the family as usual. She then asked me to get something from the kitchen, and again I did not hesitate as it was something, she would normally tell me to do. What I was not expecting was to see my father standing in the middle of the kitchen. I stood there and cried tears of joy, but suddenly all these mixed emotions came over me and I felt anger and sadness all in one. I was just fifteen years old at the time and I just remember holding him so tight and not wanting to let him go. The moment was indescribable. I had so many questions in my head and I was very overwhelmed to see him. It was a difficult time in my life, because just as one parent had reappeared in my life, the other parent was not around. I honestly didn't know how to feel, because as soon as I felt joy in my heart, I also felt my heart hurt. Due to family issues, my mother was also going to be absent for a while. But then my dad showed up. Deep down my only concern was that my dad would step up in that season and become the father I needed him to be, and to step up in his role, which he did within the season. But little did I know that the bond that I tried to fix was going to be cut loose again, and this time not by my father.

The year after I turned sixteen, I had a sweet sixteen birthday party which I will never forget, I had so much fun! Right, it's my sweet sixteenth birthday party and my mum dropped the news and told me we were moving to the UK? My initial thoughts were moving. UK? What? Why? How? When?

It took my mum just less than six months to sort out a college and get our things moved over to the UK. Every summer we went to Ghana for the holidays but that particular summer holiday in Ghana was short all of a sudden. The six weeks I was used to in Ghana seemed like two weeks because I knew after that holiday, we were moving directly to the UK. I knew NO ONE! To me it felt like I was moving to a foreign country, even though the UK was in Europe. The UK was just a strange country to me, a strange land. I had to adjust to everything. First of all, the roads were different, and everything was on the opposite side. Also everyone spoke English which was weird as I was used to the Dutch language. I was used to our Euro currency which was Guilder back then and was changed in 2001. Suddenly, I had to deal with British Pounds and leave my childhood memories back home just like that? All because my mother decided to move to a foreign country without considering my feelings. It was all too much for me and before I moved to the UK, I did not do well in my secondary school exams, as the transition was tough on me. I just had my fingers crossed and kept hoping to still get into college with my grades to do the course.

Great news: I got into the college of my choice and got the course I wanted to study, which was Travel & Tourism. Starting college was overwhelming. I was shy and confused but on that same day I met someone who also was born and bred in the Netherlands like myself and who spoke Dutch, that was a huge relief and it helped me enjoy my time in college. As I settled in at college, I made friends and was starting to get used to London and the lifestyle. However, I did miss Amsterdam a lot and I was happy I was able to go there every time I had a holiday from college. During the summer of 2008, I remember coming to Amsterdam and spending like six weeks at my uncle's place. After my holidays were over I went back to London, my mum finally moved into her own apartment with me after living with relatives since moving to Lonon for almost a year. Housing was not as easy as people thought, and I was happy for us to be in our own apartment.

October 2008 was a season which changed my life unknowingly. I came home late from school after spending time with my friends. When I walked into the house my mum called me and when I got to her room, she was seated on her bed with the lights off, which was particularly weird. I knew right then and there that there was something wrong. For a split second I pretended not to know what landed me in this situation, but deep down I already knew what she was going to say. It was up to me to act accordingly. All I could think to myself was how did I get here, and, how do I continue? A simple Friday evening that changed and shook my world.

EDITH'S GOLDEN JEWELS

Psalm 119:11

"I have hidden your word in my heart that I might not sin against you."

This was the first bible verse I recited and will never forget. My younger self knew about God , yet did not do as God said. I had his word in my heart ,yet I was sinning. But one thing I always knew was when times got hard, I prayed, they were short prayers but He listened. He made a way and He made sure I was fine again. Thank You God for holding me and protecting me at all costs even though I did not know it at times.

BRIANNA'S ACKNOWLEDGMENTS

This one's for you.
Your growth, strength, and love will be a catalyst for the world
You're healed
B.

7

BRIANNA FLETCHER – LOSING MY IDENTITY BEFORE I FOUND IT

LOSING MY IDENTITY BEFORE I FOUND IT.
Humbled.

When my dear friend asked me to be a part of this book, I was super excited yet extremely frightened. My original idea was to write a short excerpt giving advice on self-love and self-growth in order to find one's life purpose. That idea quickly went out the window when I began writing. I found myself being overwhelmed by emotions and realised that I was writing this to my younger self. I wanted to tell young Bri, everything will be okay, and every hardship will be a lesson that she will grow and flourish from. Writing this excerpt was therapeutic and healing for me, I say all this to say: come journey with me as I heal younger Bri, and I pray that it blesses and heals you too.

Let me set the scene for you: I was born and raised in New Jersey to Caribbean-American parents alongside my twin brother. My childhood was very normal and flourishing and for that I'm grateful, but I struggled with finding my identity and my true purpose that wasn't attached to what my parents or society wanted for me. I know I'm not alone when I say, my parents wanted to "plan my life". Elementary school is when I noticed that my life essentially was not my own and that my parents were very overbearing. It started with me looking a certain way, playing a certain sport, being a part of certain school academic programs, you name it and they wanted to have an input in everything. They wanted me to be their idea of "perfect." This would bring on a world of hurt and low self-esteem that they unintentional instilled in me. I would go to school and I can recall being the "perfect student"- I mean I had to be. I observed that if other students approved of me, then I would get asked to sit at their lunch table, picked to play on their kickball team at recess, and get invited to sleepovers (that I couldn't go to because, you know Caribbean parents don't play that sleeping at other people houses they don't know). At school I was also the teacher's pet, and I would strive to get good grades because I loved when my teacher bragged to my parents about how well I did in class. The feeling of being praised for being perfect was so satisfying; I wasn't even ten years old when I marvelled at the idea that all I had to do, was arise and excel at my parents' expectations, and life would be smooth and everyone would like me. How awesome, right?! Wrong! Huge problem and very detrimental to my self-worth and self-growth and it began to hurt me as a teenager.

High school was good to me, very normal. I was a cheerleader, competitive and trained dancer, on the track team, class treasurer, writer for the school newspaper, a part of the yearbook committee plus I babysat some of the neighbourhood kids. As you can see, your girl was busy. My schedule was packed. was always on a tight timeline to make sure I stayed on track with my afterschool commitments, and I began to feel burnt out by my third year of high school. I would tell myself, "you have one more year under your parents' supervision, then you'll be out on your own at college and be free." Wrong, and I'll tell you why. I would go to the college that they wanted me to go to and probably study the career I thought they would be proud of, but I was mentally exhausted and I didn't want to make a decision with them in mind. I just wanted to be happy and do what was best for me. So, in high school, when it was time to make a decision as to where and what career I would study, I took a stand and did what felt right for me. I sat my parents down and told them what I wanted. What I wanted was to attend college in Boston, Massachusetts and I wanted to be a journalist and cover entertainment news, and to my surprise they were receptive. I couldn't believe how cool and calm they were about my decision. I remember being so nervous because I didn't want to disappoint them, but the weight I carried with me since I was a child of being their "perfect child" was just too heavy to bear. Now, don't get me wrong, I don't want you to feel pity for me as if I grew up in a horrible household. No, I just grew up in a very strict Caribbean-American household with parents that wanted me to be the absolute best I could be. As I progressed and graduated from high school, preparing to go to college, I finally felt free and felt like I was "myself". But what exactly did that mean? I'll tell you what I thought it meant: finally I was doing what I wanted to do, I was making my own decisions and my parents were okay with it. How could I not rejoice and go to college happy? I literally prayed to have more freedom to think for myself and at seventeen years old I thought I obtained that. I didn't realize that yes, my parents gave me freedom to make my own decisions, but because of years and years of being a follower I didn't really know who I was. The summer of going to college I was depressed, confused and scared. I had spent my entire life being who others wanted me to be, and I told myself I didn't want to go to college a mess. There's so much pressure going to college; first time living on your own, for some people living in a different state away from your childhood friends and family, being "the new kid" all over again and formalising a plan for your future because whether you believe it or not, college is the beginning of the rest of your life. I can go on and on about the pressures of going to college, but can you imagine all this going on in my head? What would you do if you were in my shoes? I'll tell you what I did, I did what I knew best, I studied and researched the college scene and Boston culture and I transformed into the girl I saw on the internet. Yup, you read that right, even though I wanted to find myself, know myself, love myself, and live the life I wanted to live –I was just too scared. I was comfortable being who others wanted me to be, so I went to college with that mentality, but would it last? My college years, I experienced a major moment that would shift the rest of my life.

BRIANNA'S GOLDEN JEWELS

"Honour thy father and thy mother: that thy days may be long upon the land which the LORD thy God giveth thee."
   Exodus 20:12, KJV

I obeyed my parents and followed their directions over my life because I was instructed by the Lord; I didn't want to disappoint him or my parents.

"Write the vision
   and make *it* plain on tablets,
   that he may run who reads it.
   3 For the vision *are* yet for an appointed time;
   but at the end it will speak, and it will not lie.
   Though it tarries, wait for it;
   because it will surely come,
   it will not tarry.
   4 "Behold the proud,
   His soul is not upright in him;
   But the just shall live by his faith.

Another scripture that really stuck with me and propelled me to really find myself was in the book of Habakkuk 2:2.

   When I made the decision the as to where I would go to college and what I would study that was truly the beginning of my journey. I had quiet time with God and craved to find my own voice and purpose, so I meditated on the book of Habakkuk to guide me.

NATHALIE'S ACKNOWLEDGMENTS

I would like to say a big thank you to my amazing parents and immediate family for all their love and support over the years. I love you all so much.

I would also love to remember my late husband who was an amazing husband and father. We shared an amazing bond that I will forever miss. Continue to rest in eternal peace my love.

I would also like to say a big thank to Abigail Mensah for giving me this opportunity to share my story. You are the light that the world needs at this time. God bless you.

8

NATHALIE WANOGHO – UNIQUE

Unique.

My name is Nathalie Aghogho Wanogho. I was born and raised by my parents in the United Kingdom. I am the eldest of three children. My father is originally from Nigeria, located in the western part of Africa and my mother is from Martinique, in the West Indies. I mean would you not agree with me, when I say I come from two of the most beautiful countries?

Even though my parents come from different countries, I would say my father's culture played a big part in my upbringing. From the food we ate to the way we communicated with those around us. Sometimes I sit down and laugh at the things I would complain about as a child. For instance, whilst most of my friends would boast about their parents cleaning their room, ironing their clothes and going out with their friends every weekend, that was not the case with me.

In the African culture, we are taught hard work and resilience from a young age. For example, I would be expected to wake up early on Saturday mornings to clean the house and prepare for the day ahead. I would get so upset and think about why I was not enjoying the way my friends were. However, I would always get on with it without expressing my inner most frustration. I mean, sleeping over at a friend's house was non-existent, hanging around on the street I would never dare do etc. Although I grew up in a strict home, we did have enjoyable times together, for almost ten years we used to play badminton as a family, though it was a 6AM start, I really miss those times.

Little did I know that this was all training for what was to come in my life. Sometimes I find myself doing things and having flashbacks of those moments I was at home doing the same thing with a frown on my face. God always has a way of preparing you for what is to come. This is how I learnt that whatever season you are in, embrace it and learn through the process as you do not know when you will need those skills. You also don't want to be in the position where you have regrets about not taking advantage of a time in your life, that would have prepared you for your current season. Looking back, I am so grateful for the way my parents raised me.

In 2005 I had the privilege of going spending Christmas in my fatherland, Nigeria. I was

at the age where I was able to appreciate and enjoy my environment. It was an experience that changed my life. Even though I visited Nigeria when I was 2 years old, I felt like it was my first time visiting.

I will never forget our journey from Lagos to Benin. We got stopped several times by the police for absolutely no reason. I would get so fearful that it would spiral out of control, but my dad had this way of communicating with them and they would quickly let us go. We came to a point where there was a crowd of people with leprosy hiding in the bushes. As we were driving past, I made eye contact with a little boy who looked frail with hands that were eroding due to the disease. He began to walk on the road toward our direction. My side window was down so I began to raise it as he slowly approached. A tear of sorrow came dribbling down my cheek. I felt a deep sense of sadness. How could a child so young be going through such a thing? Life is just not fair.

· · ·

One of the things that amazed me about the people is that, even though the poverty is widespread, people are still so happy and optimistic. Children are full of life. One of my best moments there were the celebrations leading up to Christmas and the day itself. Everywhere was alive: houses were open, music was playing, food was in abundance and families were together and united. Especially coming from the UK, it was a culture shock to see how differently Christmas was celebrated but I embraced it and made the most of it. It must have been one evening when everyone was asleep, that my younger sister and myself sneaked out to a house not far from where we were staying. Thinking back, I don't know how we were so brave to sneak out without the fear of being caught. Our cousins were there with their friends, so we felt safe. We enjoyed the night with music, dancing and food.

I also had the privilege of spending a lot of time in France, where my mum was brought up. I always ask myself where my love for Zouk music came from. Zouk music is a popular dance music associated with the Caribbean islands of Guadeloupe and Martinique. It is a blend of a variety of Caribbean, African and North American music styles. Sometimes when I am listening to the music and close my eyes, I remember the times when we spent Christmas in France. The smell of my grandparents' food, the conversations and the laughs we had. I would remember my grandfather and grandmother dancing in the living room, the small Christmas tree quietly positioned in the corner of the living room.

From a young age I spent my school holidays in France with my mum's parents. My mum, my siblings and I would travel to Calais via the ferry, where my mum would drop us with at her brother's place. I mean I am just so grateful that I was able to spend time with my grandparents. My siblings and I had the privilege of attending summer camps whilst being in France. I loved the time spent with my grandparents.

· · ·

Fast forward to the end of my primary school life and moving onto secondary school. I was so nervous and anxious about starting secondary school. I was not sure what to expect. I was afraid of not fitting in and letting my family down. The first secondary school I attended was awful, I mean teachers did not turn up, students would hang out in the corridors with no care in the world, and there was no structure, nothing. I remember the first day I started, I felt like I had entered the London dungeon. The corridors were cold, the walls were plain, and the classrooms had a gloomy and cold feel to them. On top of feeling terrified about starting secondary school, I also had to deal with the most uncertain and unwelcoming first day. I felt so lost. In my first class the teacher seemed more interested in the time just going by quickly than paying attention to these small human beings who have just entered probably the scariest chapter of their child-hood. I thought to myself, "How am I going to achieve my GCSE's in this environment?" There was no hope. My peers didn't seem to have even realised what was going on, and I didn't want to say anything and stand out to then become the class enemy. I just couldn't see a future for myself in this kind of environment.

When I got back home, I was not sure whether to tell my parents or just see how things go. I thought to myself okay, it's the first day maybe my nerves are clouding my judgement. So, I left it and reluc-tantly made my way to school the next day. I was so scared I could feel my heart rate increasing.

At that time, my mum was working at a secondary school in Bromley. It must have been after a week that I just could no longer keep it to myself and mentioned to my mum what I had been experi-encing for the past week. Without any hesitation, the next day, my mum spoke to the headteacher in her school about the situation, whether there was a possibility that I could be offered a place. I was so happy when I got back from school and my mum told me I had been accepted into her school. There was still a sense of fear because I would be entering the school as the 'new girl'.

So, it's now my first day again in another school. All eyes are on me, I am getting checked out from head to toe. As I walk into the class for the first time, the teacher introduces me as the new girl, and I notice a mixed reaction from everyone. There were the ones who were happy to have someone new coming in, the ones who were apprehensive and then those who did not even care. You could see that friendship groups had already been made by the groups everyone was sitting in. I was worried that I would somehow have to find a group that would allow me to tag along. I was not sure where to sit, so I quickly found an empty seat where I could just sit and be invisible. I remember once the class was finished, a bunch of girls came up to me and said they would look after me. I was so happy. What a difference from where I was coming from.

Throughout my school life, I found myself doing things to please my friends just so that I could fit in and be accepted. I was also picked on and bullied for my weight, surname and a tooth gap. O
ne day I was in class feeling so deflated and frustrated with the way certain individuals were treating me in class. I just sat there quiet with my head in my hands. I totally didn't want to be there. I was just feeling so fed up and frustrated by the entire name calling. One of my classmates, who usually found pleasure in upsetting me with his hurtful words, shouted out to me and I just got up from my seat and ran towards him with so much rage in my heart. Till today I can't remember how I got from my seat to the end of the classroom so fast. I just could not take it anymore. I didn't care about the consequences. I only wanted to be left alone and seeing that my silence was being taken for weakness, I simply lashed out. The teacher was not happy at all but the luck I had was that a few of my classmates had witnessed on a few occasions how this boy was bullying me. So when it came to me being sent to the Head of Year's office, I had witnesses that could back up my story when I was explaining to my teacher how I was being bullied by this boy.

From that day my nickname was BRUZZA… (Pronounced bruise-er) but please do not think that it meant I was going around beating people up. I must say there was a bit of me that loved the fact that I was given a nickname, when Bruzza was called you knew it was me, but silently inside, the name was not what I wanted to be associated with. I thought, well I am not really a Bruzza so no biggy. Thinking of it now, only just a year ago I was in the petrol station and I heard 'BRUZZA'. I was like huh, no I must be hearing things, I mean I was a little tired so I thought to myself maybe I am hearing things. Then I heard it again and I turned to the direction of the voice, and there I saw a friend from secondary school. We both just couldn't stop laughing.

One of the things I really miss about school is the team sports. I was part of the netball team and was selected to partake at national summer athletics to compete in Shot Put and Discus. We would compete with other schools in the borough which I absolutely loved. I was also coached outside of school for Shot Put and Discus, but unfortunately, I had to stop and focus on my education. I felt a sense of loss and disappointment because it was my passion and I was very good at it. It was something that I saw myself doing for a long period of time.

My friends and I always got on the bus home together. That day we decided to sit upstairs. As I walked up the stairs and reached the top, I noticed a bunch of boys at the back. I silently said to one of the girls "Let's go downstairs" but my suggestion was ignored. I walked behind the girls and sat down quickly. I felt shy, only God knows why. After a while we all got talking and laughing. When one of the boys shouted out towards us, trying to get our attention:

'Hey you.'

'Me?'

'Yes you.'

'Ohhh me..'

I couldn't believe he had chosen me to speak to out of all us.

I mean ladies, you know that feeling when you first get noticed by a boy, it's like you are on top of the world, and you feel a sense of belonging and love. The funny thing about it is that my parents showed me a love that was unconditional; however, this was unseen and discarded by my young mind thinking I had turned into a big woman.

Fast forward to a few years later, did I drop the biggest bombshell to my father? Not just any father…. an African father.

NATHALIE'S GOLDEN JEWELS

What would I say to my younger self?

You were born different. You were born unique. There is no one else out there like you. Stop comparing yourself to your peers. Stop being pressured by your peers to do things that contradict your beliefs. Stop looking for acceptance in the eyes of those who do not respect your values. The world is waiting for you to blossom into the flower you were born to be. Everyone has their own unique identity which comes with different interests, skills, talents and gifts. This is the only way to be able to secure your own path and destination. Things may seem hard, but the hardest thing is when you are so consumed by distractions you miss your time and your unique opportunity to evolve. You are a beautiful flower that will get bruised or broken in a few places but with some sunshine (your positive energy) and consistent watering (positive people around you and what you tell yourself) you will grow new and stronger leaves and petals that are more beautiful than the ones that fell off. Most importantly, listen to those who want the best for you and that have been there and done that. As a young girl I understand you may want to be the popular one, the girl everyone wants to hang out with at school. But let me tell you this, the best way to shine and be noticed is to be your authentic self.

What I would say to my young self

- Push yourself out of your comfort zone.
- Enjoy school and make the most of every opportunity that arises. i.e. leadership roles within school (head girl/ prefect)

- Stay focused on your studies.
- If you are being bullied, it's not you. The bully is insecure, unhappy and probably wants something that you have.
- Ask your teacher questions when you are struggling in class and out of class.
- Listen to your parents, as they are speaking from a place of love and experience. If you do not understand, ask.
- Do not do things to please your friends to feel a part of the group. True friends do not pressure you into doing things you are not comfortable with.
- Focus on what you are good at/passionate about and not what others are doing. But also work on what you are not so good at to allow yourself to grow.
- Do not entertain attention from boys, as it is a distraction. There is a season for everything.
- Enjoy and make the most of your school days. You are only in school for a short amount of time.
- Take on opportunities: i.e. leadership roles within school (head girl/ prefect)
- Do not entertain attention from boys, as it is a distraction. There is a season for everything.
- Avoid peers who discourage

MONICA'S ACKNOWLEDGMENTS

I would like to thank God first and foremost for brining me this far. The trials kept coming, but I hardly complained, as I knew You would not give me anything that I could not handle. Thank You also for Your favour and for blessing me in the most incredible way.

Thank you to my Mum for always being my number one cheer-leader. We have been through it all, but God kept us going and through the trials we have the most amazing relationship. Thank you for all that you do with Amari and with all the sacrifices you have made for us. You are an amazing Grandmother.

Thank you to my son Amari; you have been my driving force. God knew you were coming so He made sure I was prepared before you arrived. I am ever so blessed to call you my son. Thank you to my brothers Kwame, Jerry, Cecil and Julian. We have had our ups and our many downs, but through it all I've come out stronger and wiser than ever before.

Thank you to all my friends and family that have helped and supported me on my journey, even those who were in my life for a season. We did not meet by mistake; I am grateful for the impact you had on my life during that season.

Lastly, thank you to my Dad. Thank you for coming back into my life and teaching me so much. I made a promise to finish what you started and that was to continue to leave a legacy. I will continue to make you proud. This one is for you.

Love, Monica x

9

MONICA FRIMPONG – BATTLING REJECTION

B attling Rejection
   My dad was the hardest working man I knew; he was the realest hustler. He was handsome, charming and very well-educated. Everyone loved to be in his presence. I was always a daddy's girl. I loved my mum don't get me wrong, but I had *so* much love for him. My family dynamic was probably the perfect family setting. It was my mum, dad, my eldest brother and me. My mum and dad moved from Ghana to the UK in the late 70s. They settled in an estate in Peckham, South London. When I was born, we moved to a predominantly white area, we were the only black family on our road that had a mortgage in the early 80s. It was the best house I've ever lived in and we had the best times. My brother and I would play in our big garden, we had a swing, a slide and back in those days, we had a seesaw. I cannot complain, we had a great upbringing in the early stages. My mum would make sure the home was taken care of. The house was always clean and food was always ready on the table. Life was really good; I barely saw my parents fight; they were like the perfect couple.

My dad was scheduled to leave for Ghana for a business trip, back then he was a well-known high-life music producer. He produced songs for artists such as Thomas Frempong, Kakiku (KK) and Kantata to name a few. I was around five or six years old at the time, but this time around when he left, he was gone for longer than usual. I had a tap and ballet class one evening, Mum said Dad was coming back today to take me. I remember being dressed and ready, kneeling on the couch looking out of the front room window. I remember like it was yesterday. I waited and waited, and he never came. I was so upset for days wondering why he didn't come back for me. Looking back at it now at the age of 36, I realise that I was going through the first stages of rejection.

I had no idea at the age of 5, that my parents were having problems and were about to get a divorce. My Dad was gone for months on end, but mum acted like he was away on business, when the fact was that he was away with his new family in Ghana. As it turned out, he found someone else much younger than my mum and they were having a child together.

Mum was struggling to keep up with the mortgage repayments. Her only option at the time was to rent out the three bedrooms upstairs and move the three of us into the living room. My mother was a trooper; she held it together for us. She never complained, nor did she show any sign of weakness or defeat. Now I know where I get my strength and resilience from, and it's from her for sure. Eventually, Mum couldn't keep up with the mortgage repayments, and we ended up becoming homeless. We moved into a hostel in Wimbledon not too far from where we lived in Norbury.

Imagine just living in a box room with three people, it was a very dark period for us, yet again, mum never complained and got on with it. My mum was getting back on her feet, she found new love with a family friend whom I was familiar with, and he was a 'favourite Uncle'. Finally, Mum was offered a new flat and surprisingly my 'favourite uncle' also moved in with us. It all happened very quickly; she never told us he was moving in, there was no conversation. He was really nice and caring at the very beginning, but as soon as my baby brother was born, everything changed. I became invisible, I felt rejected, AGAIN. He made it quite clear that I wasn't his daughter. He would put me down; tell me how stupid I was. I really believed I was stupid. I would never put my hand up in school to answer questions even if I knew the answer. I would always doubt my ability, which was due to the negative influence of my stepdad. My mother never came to my defence as she knew how bad his temper was and how abusive he could get, and she didn't want to cause any trouble. So, she allowed him to treat me the way he did. I really wished back then that my mum would have stuck up for me and put us first, but in her defence I understand why.

When the last born came things got even worse. My stepdad favoured him more as he was born with complications which almost cost him his life. Imagine having such a great stepfather and daughter relationship only to feel left out and rejected once again. "Why wouldn't he love me like his own?" I would always question myself. Am I not loveable? I was looking for love in all the wrong places.

I started getting into relationships with guys at a very young age. I was looking for validation, for someone to love me. I looked older than my age; I was attracting older men and guys who were a few years older than me. Looking back at it now, it was not the type of love God had for me. This was not love! This was abuse. Sadly, I didn't know the difference between the two. Deep down I believed these men showed me love, that they cared about me, but the truth was I was just fulfilling their needs and egos. The men would eventually leave or continuously cheat on me. I was battling with the spirit of rejection. All I have ever known since the age of 5 was rejection.

I met a guy on my lunch break whilst on work experience. Little did I know that this guy was going to manipulate and take advantage of me. I was sixteen at the time and he was in his early twenties. There was something about him that attracted me to him, he was a bad boy and didn't have many prospects but he had so much charisma (the complete opposite to what I now seek in a partner). This guy dipped in and out of my life for many years and I was just letting him. I then found out he was seeing another girl from my school, who was a year younger than myself. I could not believe it, I was distraught. I knew then that he had other motives. I was so naïve in thinking he had feelings for me. All the red flags were there. He had zero respect for me, but as I was seeking validation, I thought the affection I was receiving was some type of love and it wasn't. Many years later when I tried to break up with him, he came to my house at night and slashed all four of my car tyres just because I missed his phone calls. I was fast asleep so how could I have heard? I knew then he was dangerous, and I wanted out. I decided then to make the decision and slowly remove him out of my life and so I did. I was scared but I had to get out as I didn't want to stick around to see what else he was capable of. I stopped all contact with him, and he just stopped calling. But whenever he would see me out and about, he would try and worm his way back, I knew better and kept it moving. I just wanted to focus on myself and my studies. I knew then, getting older, that I deserved better.

If I could talk to my younger self, I would tell her how worthy she is and to never doubt herself. I would tell her to stop looking for love in all the wrong places and exercise patience, as true love will find her through Christ.

I was 17 and studying Business & Finance in college. It was during this time that my father slowly started to come back into my life. My mum, on the other hand, wasn't happy. I think she felt like I was betraying her in some way. I wasn't, I just missed my dad, despite him leaving the way he did. I was happy to have him back and rebuild from where we left off. It was like he never left to be honest. After college, I would go straight to his office and just catch up and hang out with him and talk economics and politics. He loved helping me with my assignments and I was just grateful for finally spending time with him. I was finally getting the love and attention I desired from him.

I was getting ready to apply for university. I got the grades that I needed to get into De Montfort; I was finally growing up and moving away from home for the very first time. My dad was busy with work at his legal firm, so I just got on with my application. My mum was not involved with the process as she didn't understand it fully. I was attending a university, that was all that mattered to her. Luckily for me, my uncle volunteered to assist me to visit the university so that I could enrol. When we got there, to my horror I found out that when I had applied for university it seems as though I forgot to apply for accommodation. University was commencing in less than two weeks; I couldn't believe what I was hearing.

My stress levels were at an all-time high. What was I going to do? And how was I going to find accommodation in less than two weeks? We came back to Leicester and found a shared house just in time. It wasn't what I expected but I had to make it work. I started university; I met some amazing friends. I decided over the weekend I was going to visit my friends who went to Luton University. All I remember was packing my hair tongs and jewellery in a Sainsbury's bag. I took the train and off I went. I met my friends, they kept asking if I was OK, I felt fine, but they didn't seem to think so. A few hours later I see my dad pull up, my friends had called him. He looked sad and concerned and took me home back to London. All I remember was waking up in a hospital room, I had been admitted.

Monica's Golden Jewels
    Advice:

Love yourself first before you encounter any relationship. If you do not love and respect yourself, how will you allow anyone to respect and love you? Ask yourself, are they respecting you? Are they treating you right? Do you see any red flags? If you answer yes to more than one, then my advice would be to walk away and value yourself first. Take care of number one, you!

Make sure you take time out for you. Read, meditate, and listen to music, anything to distract you from the negative vibes around you.

Always find a way to talk about any issues that you are going through. Issues that you are finding difficult to find the answer to. Always seek council from God first and listen to His instructions, be obedient. Find at least one or two people that you can gain wise counsel from. Remember, not everyone has your best interest at heart, so pick wisely too. It's OK to ask for help, don't feel like you are alone.

You matter and you are loved sis.

Sis!

Be strong and courageous! Do not be afraid or discouraged for the Lord your God is with you, wherever you go.

Joshua 1:9
This verse got me through everything. It will help you to, have FAITH.

ABRAFI'S ACKNOWLEDGMENTS

I would not have learnt much about life if it had not been for my family, especially my dad. I thank God for instituting them to guide me in my childhood years and in my walk on earth to become a woman of virtue. The discipline, the talks and advise given to me by my dad have carried me throughout my life and I am proud of the woman I am becoming. Thank you, guys!

ABRAFI AHMED – MY TRANSITION

My Transition.
The face staring back at me from my mirror is unfamiliar, yet I know it is mine. It feels like me, even if I still fail to recognize myself sometimes (Jeremiah 1:5). My name is Amina Abrafi Ahmed. Born on the 25th of October 1991 to a beautiful Muslim family; my parents, my two brothers and my sister. I am the last born. According to my parents, at a young age of two, I was normally found in a corner, busily playing on my own, reading or eating (making a mess usually). I was raised by parents that have high expectations of values, principles and having goals. I was born in a small mining town called Obuasi in the Ashanti Region, Ghana. It has been one of the best places I have lived in my entire life. I had free access to amenities, education and sporting activities such as lawn tennis, badminton, cricket and swimming. Moreover, living in the same community with expatriates and playing with their children, introduced me to learning the perspectives of people from different walks of life at an early age.

Growing up, my first brother, who is five years older than me, taught me how to do most of the chores such as washing up and cleaning. My dad used to bathe my sister and me and dress us up. I still remember the days when he had to brush our hair with tears in our eyes. He also helped my siblings and me with our homework. My dad was quite tough on us when it came especially with homework; we were expected to think on our feet. Because of this we had to place the multiplication table on the refrigerator to learn. We used to do this before my dad returned from work. My mum on the other hand did most of the cooking at home and grocery shopping. She owns a school which runs from primary to junior high. I was usually the first student to get to my class, unless I was ill or could not go to school, and this earned me a compound overseer position in primary.

I may look like I had the perfect childhood, but I had some issues I could not talk openly about, such as my faith, sex and taking decisions. Being raised in an Islamic background, I was expected to dress modestly, including wearing a hijab. As a young girl growing up, I wanted to be trendy and follow the latest fashion, which my parents were not pleased with. I used to pack extra shoes especially when they were new because I wanted to show them off in school and on weekends. When going for extra classes, I used to pack makeup and extra clothes to change at my friend's. I quite remember I accidentally left my extra shoes in my dad's car sometime; he saw them and got mad at me. I was punished by being whipped. I changed my method of taking my extra shoes to school; I used to hide them in my locker at school. I guess I was not that naughty.

Moving to junior high, I made friends with a lot of boys because I felt girls were dramatic. I kept things to myself a lot. Some of my male friends developed interest in me and used to call the landline at home, most times after school and in the evenings. My dad was not happy about that as when he happened to pick up the calls and it were my male friends, they would hang up the call. I was whipped for that as well. My mum made a complaint to my school director (they were good friends) and my male friends were called out at an assembly and warned not to call my house again. It was really an embarrassing moment for me. It earned me a nickname – Coca Cola Top 8 (because the boys that used to call my house were eight in number). I was grounded for three months. I could not participate in any sporting activity in the community, as it was believed that I was going to meet them. I kept a lot of things to myself and believed in having a locked diary where I could pour my thoughts and emotions, I could not trust my family to share my thoughts with. My parents were strict, and I felt they would never understand how I felt. One day, my mum saw my diary which was unlocked. Lol! That was trouble. I had to plead with my mum not to tell my dad, but Mama did. I got lashed by my dad for having kept a diary with my thoughts. Since then, I never write my thoughts anywhere and I keep my thoughts to myself as well.

My years in senior high were one of the best. I attended one of the best girls' boarding school in Ghana, Wesley Girls' High School, at the age of fourteen (14). It is Wesleyan School and parents (irrespective of being Muslims) are made to know that the school is guided by some Christian principles, and that if any parent was not in agreement to this, they could take their ward(s) out of the school. I think that was a miracle. I made new friends and converted to be a Christian but was not bold to tell my parents about my conviction. I felt my parents would be angry at me and I might lose my privileges as their daughter, because of the unpleasant stories I had heard about people taking the decision to convert from Islam to Christianity. Early morning devotions in chapel and in dormitory gave me the urge to know more about Christ. I started reading the Bible which I had brought to school, since it was on the prospectus. Honestly, reading the Quran back at home, I did not understand it. My dad used to read chapters to my siblings and me every morning. I did not agree to some of it, but I could not voice it out because I did not want to come across as challenging my dad. I felt much peace when I read the Bible, I may not have understood all that I read but I felt this inner peace whenever I read it. I had not declared Jesus Christ as my personal Saviour, but I still yearned to know Him more. One day, a preacher visited the school and the sermon he gave really hit me. I broke into uncontrollable tears and when he called that if anyone wanted to accept Christ should move forward, I looked around to see if anyone was watching.

I was shy, I did not know what the girls (especially those my parents knew) were going to say or say to my parents. Surprisingly, I rose to the front still crying uncontrollably and that was when I accepted Christ. It was a decision I have never regretted taking. On the lighter note I could wear what I preferred but of decency in school. I learnt how to coordinate colours in wearing an outfit, arranging my clothes in my closet and how to walk and talk like a lady, just to mention a few. However, when school was on recess, I had to go back to my old self: being a Muslim, wearing clothes my dad preferred and doing things my parents wanted me to do. It was quite challenging living the double standard life.

Attending university at the age of seventeen (17) was a learning experience. That was the beginning of my partial freedom I had always wanted as a teenager. I took decisions on my own and I had the liberty to do what I wanted but not be in trouble with my parents. I had all the fun I had always wished for: wearing clothes in my style, staying out late with friends (no parents to call when you are return-ing), having makeup that I had wanted to wear that my parents restricted me from wearing, and having a boyfriend. My dad had my cousin who is a Muslim checking on me to pray and attend Islamic functions in campus. I always kept myself busy in order not to attend them. I used to secretly attend church service with my roommate. Moreover, in the latter part of my first year, I met a wonderful guy who helped me know myself better and encouraged me to talk about how I feel. Remember, I was restricted from speaking to guys at a young age, it was quite uncomfortable having him around, but he kept coming around. We hung out a lot and got to know each other better, but I hardly spoke about my thoughts because I was learning to trust him. He later became my boyfriend and we are currently still together. Heading back home when school was on recess. You can imagine! The new me....

Reflecting on my life, I feel my parents could have explained and advised the reason behind disciplining whenever they felt I was wrong. It influenced me to be an introvert. I am very conservative, and I research a lot on everything I lay my hands and eyes on, especially with the help of the internet. In Proverbs 13:24, the Bible says, *those who spare the rod of discipline hate their children. Those who love their children care enough to discipline them (NLT).* I believe every good parent wants the best for their ward, my parents disciplining me was to help me from going wayward. The grounding, the lashes (lol!) and the Quran reading was to help me to grow up to be a person with good morals. They may have done the right thing by putting me in check but was that the right way? Children and teens are continually developing their self-image, and their big reflection comes from their parents. When children trust that their parents will be kind and fair, this allows them to be open and honest, to take responsibility and do the right thing. I am more organised and have learnt more on managing a home. I believe there is always a positive side to every situation.

ABRAFI'S GOLDEN JEWELS

May God continue to protect us

BACKGROUND OF LADIES IN WAITING

L adies In Waiting (LIW) is an international women movement that was born out of sheer passion and the need to provide solutions to the various issues plaguing women in the society. LIW tackle issues like: insecurities, bitterness, abandonment, domestic violence, self-esteem issues, and promoting self-worth among women.

At LIW, we believe women who are yet to connect with their purpose are "LADIES IN WAITING".

THE FOUNDER OF LADIES IN WAITING

Abigail Ohemaa Afriyie

Abigail is a loving wife, mentor and confidant.

Abigail is an Adaptable, Driven and Sincere woman who is passionate about others.

Abigail is able to balance life as a Lecturer and a Radio presenter of an award winning innovative show on Tribe Urban Radio.

She also has a women's ministry called Ladies In Waiting, which has had international success.

Abigail Ohemaa Afriyie is an advocate of the word, and her life-style alongside her significant experiences guide her into giving much needed advice to her audience. She is an inspiration to anyone who crosses her path.

MEET THE AUTHORS

Vicky Osei

I work in Clinical Research by profession and also as an Entrepreneur. I have a passion for helping people and am I also passionate about agriculture. I believe that we are all gifted with uniqueness to play our role and that starts with believing in yourself first.

Lucy Ahatty

I am a Mother.

I work as a Senior Nurse.

I am a woman after Gods heart, a mother, a Nurse, a mentor.

As we carry scars, I believe that one should never judge a book its covers. I'm a lover of deep conversations as this is where healing starts.

My favourite quote is "They may forget your name, but they will never forget how you made them feel." — Maya Angelou

Anastasia Owusu-Dwubeng

I am a Teacher, wife and a mother with two children. I am a Christian and I believe that helping others reaps abundant blessings and favour.

My motto in life is to always remember how you started and not how you finished. Humility is a virtue.

Tina Pokuaah

Tina describes herself as an empowered woman, who empowers women, Tina Pokuaah has cultivated her skills in project development, strategic partnerships and capacity building, to become a self-driven and ambitious Project Coordinator and entrepreneur.

As a freelance VAWG psychoeducation trainer and consultant, she designs engaging and therapeutic training materials and tool kits to deliver programs on gender inequality, to both professionals and community groups. She also challenges the normalisation of violence against women and girls..

Tina is also the Creative Director and founder of Affinity Line. It'sis an apparel and accessories brand celebrating African women in history, but also inspires the modern woman to affirm her greatness, inner power and self-discovery!

In addition, Tina also co-founded 5Girls Project, a community organisation investing in the education, skills and training of girls in Ghana and in the UK.

Edith Fosuah Wiredu

I am a mother and a wife with four children. I am a blogger who writes about personal experiences on own blog called www.walkingedithspath.com. I strongly believe in doing good to others and attracting energies. I aim to help others in many ways I can.

Brianna Fletcher

Brianna Fletcher is a New Jersey native who graduated from North-eastern University in Boston, Massachusetts, where she obtained a degree in Journalism and Communications. Upon graduation, she has dibbled and dabbled in the fashion and beauty industry and in September 2016 launched her beauty, fashion, and lifestyle blog; B*THE PLUG. Brianna curated this blog to creatively express herself and inspire others to follow their dreams and achieve their goals. She continues to use her platform to write and create beautiful content. It is an honour to be a part of this book trilogy and to share her work. Please feel free to reach out to her if you found her piece compelling, would like to collaborate, or just to say hi.

Creative: Specializes in writing and journalism
    Hobbies: Fashion enthusiast and music savant
    Based in United States of America

Nathalie Wanogho

My name is Nathalie; I am a widow and a mother to three of the most adorable kids in the world.

My husband's demise re-ignited my long-held passion of becoming a nurse as I love caring for others. With the help of my mentor and friend, I have commenced my journey of becoming a nurse.

The passing on of my husband made me angry with God, but I am slowly rediscovering my Christian roots again.

One of my guiding principles is that we all deserve a helping hand.

Monica Frempong

Pen name: Monica Akua

Mother & Entrepreneur

Becoming a single mother gave me the push to birth my business. I have been self-employed for over 10 years and love the feeling of being my own boss. I love to empower and inspire women of all ages, helping them see their full potential to pursue their dreams and overcome past traumas.

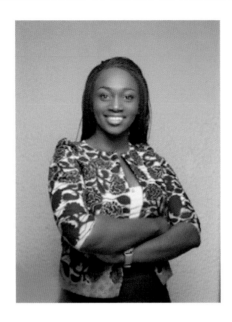

Abrafi Ahmed

I am currently pursuing a second-degree course in Sustainable Tourism in the US. I aspire to contribute my knowledge in transforming Africa with its tourism resources.

It is a blessing to be alive and I never take that for granted. I love to live a life of positivity. I set a goal for myself every month. It could be emotional, physical and psychological well-being. A little progress each day adds up to bigger results.

Look out for part two of Dear Sis
(Self-Discovery and Adventurousness)